THE NEW BREED
Living Iowa Wrestling

by
LOU BANACH
with MIKE CHAPMAN

LEISURE PRESS

A publication of
Leisure Press
P.O. Box 3; West Point, N.Y. 10996

Library of Congress Cataloging in Publication Data

Banach, Lou.

The new breed.
1. Wrestling—Iowa—Addresses, essays, lectures.
2. Wrestling—Iowa—Coaches—Biography—Addresses,
essays, lectures. 3. Wrestling—Iowa—Coaching—
Addresses, essays, lectures. I. Chapman, Mike, 1943-
II. Title.
GV1198.13.8B36   1984   796.8'12'09777   84-11217
ISBN 0-88011-258-1

Cover photo by Colbert/Edwards Tradition Photography

Cover personalities: (L to R) Front row — Barry Davis, Lou Banach, Ed Banach;
  Back Row — Jim Zalesky, Pete Bush.

Cover design: Brian Groppe

THE NEW BREED
Living Iowa Wrestling

Acknowledgements

I would like to first thank the Chapmans, Mike and Beverly; Mike for believing in my book's merit from the outset, and Bev for her important typing skills. Equally, I would like to thank my family: my parents, Alan and Stephanie; my brothers, Ed and Steve, and all my eleven other siblings for their never-ending support. Too, I would feel remiss if I did not pay gratitude to Mark Mysnyk, Mark Johnson and Tim Narey for their timely criticism. Finally, I would like to thank God for the will and talent to complete such a task.

Lou Banach
West Point, New York

Contents

Foreword

Dan Gable, Ed Banach, Lou Banach. These three wrestlers have done more to promote wrestling than any men before them. In all my years of being involved with wrestling, Lou Banach rates as one of the best big men to ever step on a wrestling mat. Had Lou Banach chosen football, I believe he would be playing in the NFL, or had he ventured into business, he would be the president of his company. I'm thankful he chose to turn his energy to wrestling. Having the skills of a middleweight and the quickness and ability of a lightweight, Lou Banach totally dominated the collegiate heavyweight scene for three years. As one-half of the best brother act in collegiate history, Lou continually sought to improve himself with his own ideas of training— which included drilling, running and weight training as well as a rigorous, hard wrestling schedule.

As a person Lou is as sincere as they come, a quality not found in many of today's top athletes.

In *The New Breed* Lou provides great insight, one no other author ever could. The high points and the bad points, Lou tells it like it is, being a national champion on a national champion team, and coached by a legend.

The road to becoming a champion isn't straight and easy, and Lou's honest approach to his book will put you in the practice room, on the mat and behind the scenes. It was a privilege to coach this man, and an honor to call him my friend.

Mark Johnson
1980 Olympic Team
Assistant Wrestling Coach,
University of Iowa

Preface

To say this book was conceived in order to pay homage to Dan Gable and the Iowa wrestling program would be to admit to a partial truth. To state that the book's purpose is to explain the behind-the-scenes functioning of the Iowa program, winner of six straight NCAA team championships heading into the 1984 tournament in East Rutherford, New Jersey, would begin to scratch the surface of its intent.

What this book offers is an in-depth scrutinization of not only Iowa wrestling specifically, but college athletics in general. By discussing and evaluating the careers of some of the most successful athletes in Hawkeye wrestling, it will provide, I hope, a meaningful insight into the world of collegiate athletics. After the completion of my five years at Iowa, I stood back and assessed the program, and came to the conclusion that any successful program resembles, in many ways, the makeup and structure of a small business—a business that learns to tolerate certain failures and inoculates its representatives against pressures that can consume them.

Pressure can make or break a businessman and a business, and it can have the same devastating effect on a college athlete or program. It is the job of the corporate leader, or of the coach, to enable his employee or athlete to cope with the increasing problems of pressure and stress that accompany him through day-to-day life. It is my fervent hope that the reader of this book will be able to learn and digest the same lessons successful Iowa wrestlers have learned in the practice room, and have learned to so efficiently put to use in the world of competition.

The message of Iowa wrestling, and this book, is not so much one of complicated rules and strategies, but rather of hard-nosed, stoic action....of discipline, adaptability and perserverance. It is a battle plan designed to combat stagnation, complacency and mediocrity.

I don't profess to know all the answers to winning or to life, of course; yet what I went through at Iowa is burned into my psyche for an eternity. At Iowa I had the opportunity to meet three great men— Dan Gable, J Robinson and Mark Johnson—men who coached wrestling, but did far more than that. They coached men on how to walk through life with head held high, shooting for goals and upholding ideals. Gable, as a wrestler and a coach, is the standard by which all others must be measured. I firmly believe that by taking part in a sport such as wrestling, and by becoming part of the overall scheme—the business, if you will—you become a better person for it, growing with the company and prospering with it as it moves on to bigger and greater challenges.

Centuries ago Plato sat in the agora (assembly place) in ancient Athens and taught that a human being is incomplete, a skeleton, unless he or she partakes of the Ideal forms of reality which exist on the highest plane. He advocated borrowing from the properties of the Good, and to grow continually. I believe those who are willing can draw from the properties offered by Dan Gable and his Iowa wrestling program, and can prosper from it. Those properties are forged in hard work and dedication, commitment and courage, and they result in phenomenal successes. You are invited to assess the Hawkeye program on the basis of what it set out to do in wrestling and what it finally achieved, and to try and grasp how it was that the Hawkeyes were able to accomplish all they did.

My parents told me in my youth that I should strive to give back something to life. I love wrestling, not as Dan, J or Mark do, perhaps, but in my own way. Wrestling has played a pivotal role in my life, carrying me from my boyhood days in Port Jervis, New York, through my college years at Iowa. It helped me to earn a valuable college education, and to learn how to accept success humbly and to grow from defeat. It is a sport that parallels life in many respects.

This book is about Iowa wrestling and success, and it is for you. As the late martial arts phenomenon Bruce Lee once said, "Take what is useful and develop from there. Discard the rest." I hope it will help you to grow and learn in some fashion, just as wrestling helped me to discover new paths and myself.

1

A PLACE TO GROW

A traveller heading into Iowa can hardly miss the big green sign with the white letters reading, "Iowa, a Place to Grow."

The state with the nation's highest literacy rate and highest ratio of colleges to inhabitants certainly does offer many opportunities to grow and expand. Just one of hundreds of examples is the sport of wrestling—and the thousands of athletes who have taken to it the last decade.

To the recently-charged wrestling fan, it may be difficult to believe Iowa has not always been a wrestling power. Though the NCAA tournament didn't begin until 1928, Iowa fielded its first team in 1911 under coach E. G. Schroeder, and it finished 0-1. It took sixty-four years for the Hawkeyes to capture their first NCAA team title. In fact, of the four Iowa colleges that have won the team championship (no other state has had more than two teams win the coveted crown), the University of Iowa was the last to do so. Tiny Cornell of Mount Vernon, just twenty miles north of Iowa City (home of the University of Iowa), captured the state's first NCAA team title in 1947 under coach Paul Scott. Iowa State Teachers College of Cedar Falls (now the University of Northern Iowa), with Dave McKuskey at the helm, followed in 1950. Iowa State University in Ames, under the direction of Dr. Harold Nichols, moved to the top of the heap in 1965. And the Hawkeyes of Iowa won their first title in Princeton, New Jersey, in 1975.

It was a long and arduous road to the top for Iowa, and was not without its pitfalls and lumps. Iowa had experienced modest success, topped off with a few peaks from time to time, under such coaches as Mike Howard and Dave McCuskey, but it wasn't until Gary Kurdelmeier arrived on the scene in 1973 as head coach that the Hawkeyes began to blossom. Kurdelmeier, an NCAA champion for McCuskey in 1958, had been an assistant for several years and had sat quietly in the background, formulating plans for the Hawkeyes' rise in the wrestling world. He envisioned many grand happenings, but it was his approach that proved essential. To Kurdelmeier, collegiate athletics was a business, and was to be approached in a business sense at all times. His goal was to analyze the strengths and weaknesses of his business, to define his goals, to lay out a specific plan of action, to market the program, and to make Iowa wrestling important to as many people as possible.

"In order to be a successful program, you have to make wrestling important to everyone—the school, the fans and the community," said Kurdelmeier back in 1978. "If it's not important, then why wrestle? If it's not important, then you might as well hold the meets in the wrestling room."

Iowa wrestling was less than successful on a financial and spectator basis when Kurdelmeier moved into the driver's seat in the fall of 1973. The offices were small and out of the way, meets were held in the tiny North Gym of the antiquated Fieldhouse, with crowds below one hundred the norm. The media were scarcely interested in the program, and fan support was almost non-existent. But Kurdelmeier envisioned growth, and was determined to change the status quo. The seed of commitment was planted.

He sought out bigger office space and got it, moving to a location down the hall nearly four times as large as the old quarters. He went after Dan Gable for an assistant coach, luring the mat legend away

Iowa coaches Gary Kurdelmeier (left) and Dan Gable watch one of their Hawkeyes in action during the 1974-75 wrestling season. Gable served as Kurdelmeier's assistant for four seasons. (Photo by University of Iowa Photo Service).

from Iowa State University, and attracting immediate media attention for his bold and audacious move. He then went one step further in the direction of Iowa State, scheduling the awesome Cyclones for the first time since 1938. He knew full well the Hawks were in for a beating in the initial meets, but he was willing to pay that price—if you want to be the best, you have to wrestle the best. Though Iowa State stampeded the Hawks in the 1973 dual meet, 29-9, Kurdelmeier was smiling on the inside with the knowledge he had helped create enough interest in the sport to attract a national record crowd of 12,000 fans.

"Before that meet we used to have just one ticket-taker on duty," said Kurdelmeier. "At that time, we really weren't selling tickets, and a lot of people were coming in the back door, free. That one meet, for all practical purposes, changed things."

The wheels of the Iowa wrestling business were set in motion. With Gable basically in charge of the practice room, Kurdelmeier went in search of promotions that would give wide exposure to wrestling. He marketed Iowa wrestling wherever possible, largely through the name of Gable. Kurdelmeier envisioned greatness for Iowa, and Gable personified it. Iowa wrestling was a business with a product—championship performances.

But there was no easy road to success. Kurdelmeier and Gable were going to have to work for every ounce of success to come their way, and they knew it. Kurdelmeier recognized the problems of stagnation and contentment, and immediately set out to stiffen the schedule, lining up meets against the best teams in the sport.

In matters of business, Iowa learned to adapt to "the system." By NCAA rules, a wrestling team is allowed to carry eleven full scholarships over a four-year period, and Kurdelmeier recognized that to get the most out of those scholarships Iowa had to land additional financial help. By splitting up the money, offering a one-third scholarship to three different wrestlers, Iowa was able to bring more candidates into the room. Iowa also found athletes who could receive financial aid, based on need, from different national agencies. Eddie, the Zalesky brothers and I were on this package program, open to everyone who qualified on a financial-need basis. And that was a key element for the athletes in the practice room, as I sincerely feel a wrestler is only as good as his workout partners. At Iowa I had six or seven different guys to grapple with, and it made a hell of a difference.

The wrestlers at Iowa were "employed" by the Iowa wrestling team, in a broad sense. Their job, aside from attending classes and earning a diploma, was to train day-in and day-out to make Iowa the very best wrestling team in the nation. Their pay came in the form of scholarships, Big Ten and national titles and the tremendous feeling of fulfillment one gets struggling his very hardest to reach a worthwhile goal.

The program is run like a successful business in that there is the need for the same type of commitment, dedication and hard work that one must have in the professional working world. But there is still another side to Iowa's success.

"It's been obvious to me that if you want to get people involved with something, you do it through kids and through love," said Kurdelmeier. Soon the Hawkeyes were sponsoring wrestling clinics for small fry on Saturdays, and parents were becoming involved.

"When kids come to a clinic they have to get rides from parents," said Kurdelmeier. "Parents got so that they would stay around and watch, or come early and watch till the end. They became wrestling fans."

At last Iowa had something to sell, and someone to sell it to. The program, through Gable's efforts, has received remarkable recognition. Gable and Ed Banach were guests on the *Today* show, and Gable has been on several national radio talk shows out of New York and Chicago. In some Iowa newspapers, *The Cedar Rapids Gazette* in particular, Hawkeye wrestlers receive as much attention as the basketball players, and their matches are treated as front-page news, with large headlines. They wrestle in the spacious Carver-Hawkeye Arena, in front of crowds that range from 4,000 for the smaller meets to a national record 15,500 for the Donnybrook meets with Iowa State.

Iowa has built a dynasty with hard work, not money. The Oklahoma schools have their oil tycoons and Iowa State a millionaire coach and other large backers to match or surpass Iowa financially. What Iowa has is a work ethic matched by none, anywhere, in collegiate sports. But Iowa doesn't look to its past; with Gable leading, it looks to its future. "My interest is in the future because I'm going to spend the rest of my life there," said Charles F. Kettering. It's a philosophy Iowa relates to very well.

There is always one more goal to achieve, one more mountain to climb. And the complaints of coaches who have lost the will to keep pace falls on deaf ears.

"Don't be concerned for what the other man has, the job he is doing," said Ken Leuer, a former Iowa 191-pound national champion (1956), now a major general in the United States Army. "Don't be jealous of his awards or accomplishments. Don't worry for tomorrow—for it will be there as sure as the sun rises in the east. Stay inside your glass, your sphere, and set your goals. Take pride in your work, yourself and your team. Do this on a daily basis. Only by working hard today will you be successful tomorrow."

Gable has issued a challenge to the wrestling world. He asks other coaches not to sit idly by and watch the Hawkeyes race away uncontested into the sunset, but to give chase—pursue and struggle to catch up, if they can. The thrill of sports is in the hunt, the chase, and not always the victory!

"Shame on anyone who begrudges Dan Gable the success he has earned," said Russ Hellickson, Wisconsin coach and silver medal winner in the 1976 Olympics, in an article in *Sports Illustrated*. "Thank God Dan chose wrestling. He doesn't seek excellence to be honored, he honors us by seeking excellence. Hold back, hell. Pour it on, Dan. We're going to catch the Hawks. Thanks for providing us our great challenge."

That's the spirit that fashioned America and made it great. That's the spirit that built the great businesses of America, and provided so many wonderful opportunities for all who dare to excel.

And that's the spirit in which this book is written. If you can learn something new, or gain some inspiration, accept the ultimate challenge, establish meaningful goals, develop the desire to commit yourself to them, then you can become a part of the new breed . . . . a breed apart. It's a breed that accepts failure only when it is productive, learns from each mistake and setback, works harder tomorrow than today. It is a breed that knows no barriers, accepts no limits, no boundaries for success, and no excuses for failure.

Follow me and other Hawks, the members of the new breed, in the pages that lie ahead. For Iowa is indeed a place to grow.

2
THE EDUCATION
OF A COACH

Eddie Banach

It has been said you can measure a man in two ways: The first is by looking at what he has already accomplished; the second is by looking at what that person is capable of achieving. One method is connected to the past, while the other looks to the future. Both have merit; both have meaning.

Dan Gable, an exception in so many aspects of his life, is here again no exception. As a wrestler he reached many lofty plateaus, winning 180 straight matches at one point, compiling a record of 305-7 in all competition and winning five national titles (two NCAA , two AAU and one Federation) and two world titles, the second at the 1972 Olympics. He has set the standard in the areas of mental toughness, conditioning and dedication to the sport. Still, this is yesterday's success, as magnificent as it is.

It is the future that Gable is concerned with now. Gable the wrestler has exited, and Gable the coach has arrived. One education has ended; the other is still under way. As a wrestler, he passed every test with flying colors, accumulating ribbons, trophies and accolades by the bushel. As a coach he has done just as well, leading his Hawkeyes to six straight NCAA team titles and fashioning a dual meet record of 122-5-2. He stands alone as the only man in wrestling history to have won 100 matches as a collegiate athlete, and 100 matches as a collegiate coach.

It is no easy task to break old habits, to forget about "me, the individual" and to begin caring just as earnestly about "them, the team." In adopting the team concept, a coach must learn to deal with as many as forty or more individuals, particularly the top ten who comprise the starting lineup. While the team concept looms large, so does the individual concept, for it is the individuals who will, collectively, account for the successes or failures of the team.

To suggest that Dan Gable made the smooth transition from wrestler to coach without a misplaced step or stumble would not only be inaccurate, but unfair. Dan Gable the coach experienced many difficult and trying days as a novice coach, but he seldom buckled or wavered. Instead, he flourished as he learned from each new experience, and eventually became a mature, totally effective coach—perhaps the most productive coach of any sport on any level in National Collegiate Athletic Association history.

Today's college wrestler, especially at the University of Iowa, is a product of 300 to 400 high school matches, and may have captured anywhere from one to four state titles. He probably has participated in at least one junior national wrestling tournament and many other summer meets, honing his skills against the best junior-level matmen in the United States. He is an athlete who is experienced, dedicated and knowledgable when it comes to wrestling.

But at Iowa, this wrestler also is his own coach, to a certain degree. Though he has the best wrestling coaching staff in America at hand, he is accountable to a very large degree for his own actions—his failures as well as his successes. He knows he can win

Ed Banach brought to Iowa all the qualities a champion needs, including a backbreaking bear hug and an unfailing belief in himself. (Photo courtsey of the *Cedar Rapids Gazette*).

if he follows the guidelines laid out for him by the coaching staff. It is a program of incredibly hard work, weight training, running, diet control, technique drilling and just plain wrestling. He becomes his own coach only when he has displayed sufficient motivation and character to serve as his own coach and his own man. It is a status that must be earned, and held.

It's a new breed of wrestler, actually, one that first arrived on the University of Iowa campus in the fall of 1978. He came to Iowa to be taught by the best, to train with the best, and to become the best.

In the process, the new breed of athletes left something behind. While learning to become a champion, he helped teach Dan Gable and his excellent assistants, men like J Robinson and Mark Johnson, how to become even better, more effective coaches than they were before. The making of champions was also, in my estimation, the education of a coach.

Ed Banach was the first of the new breed to arrive on the Iowa campus. Rugged looking and sporting a mental attitude that would overcome all obstacles, he epitomized the transition period that would challenge the emerging coach that was Dan Gable. Ed was a maverick in the true sense of the word, and brought to Iowa all the qualities a champion needs. He also brought qualities that would help his coach understand better than ever his role in athletics.

In high school in Port Jervis, New York, Ed was active in just two sports, football and wrestling. He was on the varsity wrestling team four years, and showed improvement each year—a quality that characterizes the new breed of athlete coming to Iowa. As a freshman Ed finished fourth in the sectional tournament, and narrowly missed the New York state meet. That summer, prior to his sophomore season, he began training with weights and started to develop his mental toughness, two more qualities that are essential characteristics of the new breed.

Ed was possessed by the time wrestling season rolled around. He had set his goals high and was determined to become a state champion as a sophomore, a feat almost unheard of in New York, a state that has only one class. Everyone mocked Eddie for dreaming so high and for expressing his dreams, but he was undaunted, ignoring the laughter of friends and teammates. He stuck to his goal, another sign of the new breed. When the season was over, Ed had made big strides toward his goal, yet had fallen short; he placed fifth in the New York Public State Wrestling Tournament (in the 167-pound class) held in Syracuse.

While most wrestlers would be pleased with a fifth-place finish as a sophomore, Eddie was hurting inside. He had not reached his goal, one which he sincerely felt he could have attained. He began to reflect on why he had fallen short and enlisted the aid of his high school coach, Mark Faller (now the head coach at Franklin and Marshall College), to help Ed overcome the hurdle between him and the state championship. They came to the conclusion that Eddie's biggest barriers were experience and technique; he had struggled valiantly but the wrestlers he faced at the state meet all had more experience and better technique. Mark and Eddie knew the answer was more wrestling, especially in freestyle summer tournaments. Another mark of the new-breed athlete coming to Iowa was his willingness to compete in the junior national tournament each summer in Iowa City.

That spring Ed placed second in the Eastern junior tournament and followed up by placing fourth in the junior Greco-Roman national meet in the summer. This invaluable experience helped Ed gain the runner-up spot in the state high school tournament (155 pounds) as a junior, and he went back on the freestyle circuit the summer before his senior season. He won the New York freestyle title, placed second in the Eastern junior tournament again and then took second in the junior nationals in Iowa City. He lost in the finals of the junior nationals to Colin Kilrain, a matman he would butt heads with several times during their collegiate careers when Kilrain wrestled for Lehigh University.

His senior season marked the end of the long, battle-scarred road for Ed—and the realization of his goal. He won the state high school tournament in the 167-pound class. Now he was being courted by nearly every major wrestling power in the country, and why not? Ed had everything the coaches were looking for; he was a top student, physically strong, mentally tough, highly motivated and was coachable. Though Lehigh, Oklahoma State and Oklahoma all were chasing him, Ed opted for Iowa, because, he said, "To be the best you've got to go where the best are."

His freshman year at Iowa was one of growth and dreams. While he toiled in the wrestling room, discovering the vast difference between high school and collegiate wrestling, he set his goals firmly. He was red-shirted, and used the year to improve his technique and assess his chances of becoming a four-time NCAA champion. Gable loved Eddie's attitude, his fierce competitive nature, his crushing style of attack, his relentless drive. But many of his teammates laughed at his vanity, thinking it preposterous he should dream of four national titles before he had even made the Iowa squad.

"I remember Ed used to say he would be a four-timer. He couldn't even beat Scott Trizzino or Mark Stevenson — I thought he was crazy," said Mike DeAnna.

Unscathed, Eddie plowed ahead. After his freshman red-shirt season, he entered the Federation national tournament, but failed to place. A month later, however, he finished fourth in the AAU national meet in Ames. He trained that spring and summer, his mind on the NCAA tournament that was still almost nine months away. He ran long miles, lifted heavy weights and practiced technique with the zeal of a Trappist monk. Word began to circulate that Gable had a prize recruit in the wrestling room, one who battled with the determination of a street fighter, who would do anything to win, including beating the foe into submission.

Dan and J Robinson had tried to teach Ed technique, but it was a slow and arduous undertaking. Ed's style was not one of finesse, but of rock-hard, jolting, never-say-die wrestling. A foe, to have any hope of beating him, had to build a huge lead early and then try to withstand the battering that was sure to follow in the closing minutes. Ed was a machine from the same mold as Gable himself and was capable of intimidating an opponent before the match ever began.

When the season started, he rolled over foe after foe, slamming them to the mat with vicious bear hugs and turning them with painful arm bars. He won the Midlands tournament his freshman year, and pinned Iowa State's All-America performer Dave Allen in the dual meet. He breezed through the Big Ten tournament as if it was a cakewalk, and entered the NCAA tournament with a glistening 36-3 record. At Corvallis, Ed was overwhelming. He stormed back from a 9-3 deficit to sideline Kilrain in the semis, 12-11, and then defeated Allen in the finals 16-5. There, in Corvallis, Oregon, Ed Banach had taken the crucial first step in his goal toward becoming a four-time NCAA champion. When the final match had ended, Ed turned toward his coaches and raised four fingers, signifying to the entire wrestling world what his goal was. No one was laughing anymore. Ed Banach epitomized the new breed of wrestler at Iowa, one who would claw, fight and battle his way up through the ranks in order to prove he belonged. No price was too great to be the best.

His sophomore season was more of the same for the Port Jervis express. He captured the Midlands for the second time, and took home his second Big Ten championship. He entered the NCAA championships in Princeton as the most talked-about collegiate wrestler in the country, and came away with five more victories, pinning Clarion State's Charlie Heller in the finals. Now Eddie was a two-time NCAA champion with a fabulous 76-4 record (with 32 pins) in his first two years of competition. The way seemed clear as he sought to make wrestling history by becoming the first four-time NCAA champion in the long and illustrious history of the sport. Since the first NCAA meet back in 1928, no athlete had ever been able to claim four titles, although Dick Hutton, Pat Milkovich and Lee Kemp had all come close. Ed seemed to have an excellent chance.

But it seems there is always something, or someone, lurking in the background, waiting for an opportunity to leap into the national spotlight. Ed discovered this sad fact of life, along with another, his junior year.

For the first three years (two years of wrestling eligibility and the freshman red-shirt year), Gable had very few problems with Ed Banach. He was an ideal athlete, and Dan was able to devote most of his time to the other wrestlers on his squad. But the tables turned during Ed's junior year.

The first sign of trouble came at the Midlands tournament. Ed won his third straight title at 177, but not without a tremendous battle from Mark Schultz, the Oklahoma star who had upset DeAnna in the finals of the NCAA meet the previous spring at 167. Eddie and Mark gave the crowd its money's worth, with Ed taking the win, 5-4. At the conclusion of the post-meet ceremonies, Ed told one journalist that Schultz had given him all he could handle, and added he expected the Oklahoma strongboy to be his toughest foe of the year. How right he was! In the dual meet at Oklahoma City, the two traded points with brilliant wrestling, but this time Mark ended up on top with a thrilling, last-second takedown, 10-9. Ed had been handed his first loss of the season, and his first setback in nearly two years of wrestling.

The two went separate ways in the conference tournaments, with Ed cruising to his third straight Big Ten title and Mark nipping Iowa State's Perry Hummel to win the Big Eight meet. But they were still on a collision course, destined to meet for the third time this season—in the finals of the NCAA championships in Ames.

At the beginning of the season, *Amateur Wrestling News* was among the many observers who considered Eddie a shoo-in for his third straight NCAA title. Nearly everyone had expected the first two crowns to be the toughest ones to win. But by the time the NCAA meet rolled around in Ed's junior year, the wrestling community was pretty well divided on his chances to win his third.

In Iowa City there was a strange feeling descending on the Iowa wrestlers and their fans: They were seeing subtle changes in Eddie's attitude and his preparations. The work ethic and hard conditioning by which he had become known were things of the past. Eddie was concentrating too much on pulling weight, and cutting to 177 from his off-season weight of 205 pounds was not as easy as it had been the two previous years. Ed had matured into a bigger, more powerful man, and the weight didn't come off as easily as before. He was also spending more time worrying about specific opponents, like Kilrain and Schultz, than he had in the past, and consequently he was spending less time on weight training and on staying physically tough.

In effect, Ed had become his own coach. He was a two-timer; he "knew" what to do to be successful, but his definition of success had somehow been altered. He wanted to abandon the horse that brought him the two championships and ride another horse to his third. Ed didn't want to be as physical as he had been, but rather to be more of an artful and "slick" style wrestler. Throughout the season Gable had allowed Ed to coach himself. Even after the loss to Schultz in the dual meet, Gable had not taken charge, preferring to let Ed work it out on his own, as he desired.

Driving for his third NCAA title, Ed defeated four straight foes at the NCAA meet in Ames, but he still didn't look like the Ed Banach of old. In the finals he was sluggish, weak and mentally tired. Cutting the weight and worrying about opponents had had their effect, and he was beaten by Schultz in a startling match, 16-8. Ed had been in it all the way until the very last move when, trailing 10-8, he locked up with Schultz and went for the big throw. It was the way Ed had always wrestled—going for the big move, but he wound up on his back, surrendering vital points, before he rolled through. It was over. His quest to become the first four-timer in NCAA history was finished.

Ed knew he had failed, and Gable felt he had, too. In wanting Ed to become a better technical wrestler, he had not closely monitored his condition and mental attitude. The two of them sat down after the tournament and tried to fit the pieces together. They agreed the issue wasn't who was at fault, but how could they learn from what had transpired.

The first step to be taken for Ed's final season was to take the pressure off him mentally by allowing him to compete at 190 pounds. Though the Hawks already had a returning national champion at that weight in rugged Pete Bush, the decision was that Ed would move up, and the two would decide in tryouts who would take that position into the upcoming season. But Bush was injured (by Ed) and wound up red-shirting. The 190-pound spot on the Iowa team was Ed's, and he set out to win the national title there as well.

Ed soon became his old self. He was lifting again, practicing his techniques and wrestling in the old, punishing fashion. What's more, the fire had returned to his eye.

But the fire dimmed to a flicker when he was defeated by Iowa State's Mike Mann in the 1982 Northern Open, 5-3. Mann, a talented and rugged grappler, had lost to Bush in the 1982 NCAA finals and, facing his final season of competition, was bound and determined to capture the same NCAA title that Eddie was after. They were destined to meet a total of four times during the season.

Gable stepped in. He was not willing to leave the improvement Ed needed solely in his wrestler's hands; he was determined to do all he could to insure Ed's ultimate victory. They went to work first on his attitude, trying to regain the fire, the eye of the tiger. Next, Gable began working on mat positioning, especially in reference to Mann's style of wrestling. Gable instructed Bush to work with Ed, as Bush had tangled with Mann on a number of occasions (in fact, Pete's only victory over Mann was in the NCAA finals). Gable figured Bush was the expert, and together the three of them worked on the common goal—defeating Mike Mann.

But by the first Donnybrook series of the 1982-83 season, Ed still had not improved enough. Mann, wrestling superbly, countered Eddie to perfection and worked his own offense skillfully, taking a 13-8 victory. And it was more of the same the third time they collided, with Mann posting a 10-9 victory in the last dual meet between the two titans.

The last loss to Mann had Gable upset and confused, but not for long. He reasoned Eddie would have to put himself into a total wrestling frame of mind, working as never before. The last six weeks of Eddie's career would call for a commitment from both coach and wrestler on a scale that neither had envisioned.

"Eddie Banach has meant too much to this program and to wrestling to end his career in second place," said Gable sternly to members of the news media. "If I have anything to say about it, he's going out on top."

Ed Banach and his Hawkeye teammates complete laps around the mat during a workout before an Iowa football game. The practices have attracted crowds of over 3,000 prior to football games.

The key to any athlete's success is the countless hours spent perfecting skills, and Ed Banach paid that price as well as any athlete ever could.

The new program was in force: Ed began working out three times a day, including sessions at 4:30 a.m. and at 8:30 a.m., in addition to the regularly-scheduled practice at 4 p.m. Gable was at his side, motivating him and coaching him through the exhausting, mind-draining workouts. Gable was prepared to pay the same price he was asking Ed to pay; Ed was not expected to go it alone, even in the early morning hours of the day. Both Dan and Ed had made their minds up to the fact that if Eddie was to lose to Mann for a fourth time, it would not be because he was not in the very best of shape, both mentally and physically.

In Oklahoma City, Ed and Mann easily pushed aside all other competition, heading for the final showdown. After both had scored victories in the semi-final round, the die was cast. Mann retreated to his motel room, refusing to issue quotes to the media. He needed time to prepare for his last bout with the Hawkeye. Eddie was keyed up, too, but seemed more relaxed to the outside world.

The third time wasn't the charm for Ed, but the fourth time was. Scoring the only offensive points on a perfectly-executed single leg takedown, Eddie came away with a 4-3 triumph. Though Eddie missed becoming the nation's first four-time NCAA champion, he did become the first three-timer in the proud history of University of Iowa wrestling. He also closed out his career with the most wins (141) in Iowa history, and the most pins (73). Later he was awarded the Olympia Award by the Southland Corporation (7-11 Stores) in recognition of his tremendous wrestling accomplishments, and was voted the top athlete of the Big Ten Conference, eclipsing such standouts as Michigan All-American football star Anthony Carter. The Ed Banach story had run its course at Iowa, and had moved into the history books for future athletes and fans to marvel at.

But Ed became part of something more important than just record books. He helped Dan Gable become an even better coach than he was in the fall of 1978, when Eddie first enrolled at Iowa Gable was no longer determined to categorize wrestlers in one specific mold. Gable recognized that his new-breed athletes, for the most part, could coach themselves, although he still needed to keep a very watchful eye on them. They needed freedom to experiment and grow, but even seniors needed guidance when they strayed from the path. It was this new system of coaching adopted for the new breed which would reap the greatest opportunity for success.

Gable hates to deal with "chance," and he does all he can to overcome the odds, to control them and to do everything humanly possible to make his wrestling team and wrestlers the very best. The only way it is possible is to listen to the wrestlers, observe them, get to know them individually and then translate what he has learned into hard, concrete action. But the communication alone is not enough.

Working at full speed in his style of constant motion, Ed Banach overwhelmed foe after foe. He became the University of Iowa's first ever three-time NCAA champion and set school records for most wins (141) and most pins (73). (Photo by Chuck Yesalis).

Gable actually gets down in the trenches with his boys, as he did with Ed, and demonstrates what is needed, sharing in the work and the commitment.

Ed Banach was the new bread of athlete, but Dan Gable is the new breed of coach, one who will devote the extra time, patience and understanding to the athlete. It's a breed that lives not only for the betterment of the athlete, but for the good of the sport, realizing that champions are made through equal portions of hard work, discipline and caring.

Ed Banach didn't limit his growing opportunities to athletics. He once appeared on stage in the role of a wrestler in a Shakespearean play. In the photo above, he grapples with a foe during a rehearsal. (Photo courtesy of University of Iowa).

Dave Fitzgerald

Dave Fitzgerald was not your typical athlete; he was a young guy who changed more than the season. And because of that fact, he became a challenge—a big challenge—for his coach, Dan Gable. Fitzgerald offered many talents to the Hawkeye team: He was physically mature, had a great deal of wrestling experience and, most of all, knew that to be happy in any sport—whether it be wrestling, football or soccer—he needed to work at the sport in his own way, no matter how unusual it might seem to others.

And he certainly had his own unique style. The problem was that his style was not so much one of hard work or discipline, but rather one of a carefree, day-to-day, easy-come easy-go attitude. For Gable, a wrestler who was dominated by discipline and drive, it was a style bound to pose a conflict and offer a stiff challenge to his coaching principles.

At the outset of his Hawkeye career, in the fall of 1977, Fitzgerald had all the credentials a top coach could hope for. He began wrestling as a youngster in Davenport, Iowa, and enjoyed considerable success. He attended a number of wrestling camps to hone his adolescent skills. As time passed, however, Dave changed, as is the case with any human being. Along with the change came an evaluation of wrestling, and where it would ultimately fit into his life. He tested the meaning of wrestling many times during his high school days.

While at Davenport West High School, Fitzgerald managed to carve a lofty reputation for himself, much in the fashion a bully is able to acquire a name for himself. To say only that Dave was mean, hardnosed and stubborn would not be totally fair to him, because he was raised in a manner that was, well, different. Hard work and struggle were commonplace in the Fitzgerald family. His dad, a laborer, understood life is tough, and the best way to make it through is to stare it right in the eyes and spit into its face—nothing fancy, just effective. Dave has that same attitude toward life. And a certain stubbornness.

It was a stubbornness he carried into every aspect of life, a life full of juvenile pranks, games and lessons. Whether or not he enjoyed the lessons is another story, but this fact remains: The lessons he learned growing up in a rough-and-tumble river town on the banks of the mighty Mississippi formed the character of Dave Fitzgerald.

Dave Fitzgerald came to Iowa after winning two state titles at Davenport West High School. A tough, hard-nosed competitor, Fitzgerald had to leave Iowa before finally realizing what the program really had to offer.

I first encountered Fitz at the United States Wrestling Federation Junior National tournament in the summer of 1977. I recall vividly the stern look on his face; it was the face of a cowboy—square jaw, sunken eyes and bushy eyebrows. Yet at the same time he had the appearance of a California beach bum, attired as he was in sandals and dark glasses, sporting a golden tan, his hair bleached a honey blond color. He seemed out of place and maybe out of time. Nonetheless, he was quick to show he was a hard-nosed competitor.

His rough-and-tumble lifestyle manifested itself in his wrestling. His opponents often as not came out of their matches sporting cuts, with blood dripping down their fronts, while Fitzgerald looked much the same. But it was this scrappy and determined type of wrestling that attracted Gable to him—he was one of the new-breed types the Iowa coach was seeking for the foundation of his program.

While Fitzgerald met Gable's on-the-mat criteria, it was a far different story off the mat. To be a part of this Gable breed, one needed to be a total wrestler, one who could and would train two hours in the early morning and come back for a two- or three-hour workout in the afternoon, in the heat of summer or the frigidness of winter. To accompany all the physical exercise, Gable liked to see an intense desire to wrestle, a commitment to the sport that existed deep inside the athlete and that could be brought to the surface at a moment's notice.

But in Fitzgerald's case, that was a problem. No one really knew what it was that motivated Fitzgerald when it came to wrestling.

There are a number of possibilities one can summon up when figuring what it is that motivates an athlete—there are fans, the desire for media attention, the desire to please someone and pride. Yet I believe that in Fitz's case it was something more down to earth, more primeval—more American, if you will. I think Dave was motivated by an internal drive to fight for his ground....to stick up for his rights, to protect his "turf," and even, perhaps, to stake a claim on his manhood. The Old West may be gone, but to this river-town resident the rules and principles that governed that rather lawless era are not. Gun duels are no longer possible, and bare-fisted brawling is unacceptable social behavior; so he was searching for a new method to prove himself in a constantly changing world. Wrestling is one of the last effective means for testing manhood, to find out where our values lie, and to discover who we are. It is often a cruel sport, often punishing, a sport that is not necessarily intended to be fair, but rather a device for gauging one's strengths and ultimately one's weaknesses. It looks to the very core of a man. Wrestling took Fitz on an odyssey of self discovery, and through it he found who he really was.

His search for self began to take form when he was a senior in high school, and it broadened the following summer at the national meet in Iowa City. There he finished third in the 178 weight division, behind such potential stars as Colin Kilrain and Ed Banach. But the manner in which he earned his third-place award was the vital aspect of the competition.

Fitz was clearly not the best-conditioned athlete in the field, but that is a fact of life that suits his nature. Life is, in his perspective, a battle, a fight, a scrap. We aren't always prepared for each and every battle and, because of that, life is more meaningful when tested without preparation. It is also more dangerous and more risky. But that's Fitzgerald's style—to live on the brink of failure, to dwell on the edge of success. In doing that, some of the fear of life disappears.

Fitz took third by placing himself on the brink of disaster and surmounting with sheer guts and heart the many problems presented by a lack of conditioning. It was an attitude that attracted Gable's attention, and when September of 1977 rolled around, Fitz was a Hawkeye. Yet he was not in the Gable fold; he was a Hawkeye who had his own reasons for wrestling and was in search of his own meaning of life. While he was in the midst of his journey for self realization, Gable and his coaches would be put to a similar test for their program. Fitzgerald presented them with a challenge, one that could, ultimately, be met only through an acceptance of yet another new and different breed of athlete.

Fitzgerald's chance to test his manhood came quickly his freshman year; he took his lumps at 177 pounds, while savoring a few hard-earned victories. He gained invaluable experience, however, and became the varsity 177-pounder the following season, but not without a struggle. He squared off against a grappler who had beaten him the previous summer, and the two fought with everything they had; it was a match that involved more brawn than skill, more blood than sweat. But it was the way Fitz preferred it, they way he liked it. The wrestle-off with Ed Banach was about the same as a legalized street fight, and Fitz prevailed. This was a day he could stand tall and proud, and confident. He had taken another step toward manhood. Still, the 1978-79 campaign was laced with lessons, bitter as well as sweet. For most of us, the sad or distasteful moments are the ones we cherish the least, but remember the best, and so it was with Dave.

He finished the season with a 11-10 record, and had to face a renewed challenge from Ed the following season. This time, however, the tables were turned, and victory changed sides. Ed won the wrestle-offs and became the Hawks' new 177-pounder. As Ed piled up win after win, beginning with the Midlands Tournament in December, Dave was in the midst of a long and bitter season. In the true spirit of a winner, something he had always been, Fitz wanted to wrestle, badly. He would sacrifice the food, the water, the good times with his friends to make the Iowa lineup at 167 pounds. But it was a

The weight cutting, combined with the lack of a social life and the declining grades, all became too much for him to cope with. He yearned for a cold beer, a night on the town, even a cold soda. Disillusionment ballooned, and Fitz began to seriously question wrestling and life. Like many athletes before him, he had lost the meaning of wrestling. He quit the Iowa team.

The day he quit is etched in my mind. We were to wrestle arch-rival Iowa State that same Saturday night. Fitz, exhausted and drained, walked into the dressing room, stripped and weighed himself. He was a couple of pounds over, but it was a couple of pounds he did not appear to have. He was as skinny as a refugee. His eyes were drawn deep into his head, his muscles rippled like those of a bodybuilder, and his tongue and skin must have been as dry as the Arabian desert. All he wanted was to drink a common glass of water, and to enjoy the sweet taste of fruit. But wrestling is a sport of sacrifice, and food, water and friendships are luxuries that are often cast aside in the pursuit of victory. The meet went on, but without Fitz.

Where have you gone, Dave Fitzgerald?

Hawkeye wrestler missing all week

By BOB DYER

Dave Fitzgerald on Gable's Missing List

On top of all the other problems that have beset Iowa's No. 1 rated wrestling team this season, Coach Dan Gable now has a missing wrestler on his hands.

"Do you think The Register could run a banner headline asking Dave Fitzgerald to please come home?" Gable asked Thursday.

"He's on my missing list. He hasn't shown up for practice this week and nobody knows where he's at or what he's been doing. The last thing we heard was that he was in Texas.

Fitzgerald, a junior from Davenport, was Iowa's top 177-pounder last year but this season lost his job to redshirt freshman Ed Banach. Fitzgerald was forced to cut to 167 this year to earn a berth in the starting lineup and therein Gable believes lies the problem.

"Dave thinks he's a 177-pounder," Gable said. "He's had doubts whether he wanted to continue cutting weight but he really hasn't given himself a chance

"He thinks he's a loser and so are the team likes him. That's not true. This is the first time since Dave's been here that he's really started to come on and had people talking about him. Then he packs his bags.

Fitzgerald has an 11-4 record this season and placed sixth in the rugged Midlands tournament. He failed to make weight Saturday and missed Iowa's 33-7 victory over I.wa State.

Gable said Fitzgerald did not call to him before earning the team.

Dave knew I'd talk him out of it Gable said. We'd welcome him back now. We need him. I'd rather have him with us than on the streets.

I don't know whether he's ever going back to school. Even if he doesn't say wrestling anymore he can stay at Iowa if he want.

THIS SEASON has been one of constant turmoil for Iowa and the Hawkeyes will meet second ranked lehigh at Iowa City Saturday night.

Iowa's other top two 167 were sidelined. Then Fitzgerald had a premature exit.

And the former Olympic champion explained Tuesday that he's dropping freshman Jeff Kerber .24 from the lineup and will replace the former four time state champion from Emmetsburg with another move 7 in Russ of Iowa City.

Kerber 26-0 as a prep had a 21-4 mark this year and has dropped six of his last seven bouts.

We're not giving Kerber a rest yet a rest from dual meets said. We're going to work him over than he has ever wrestled before in practice.

Kerber's physical stage has been weak going, enough from winning to school. He's got to realize that smaller high school men compete in college at a better He's not ready for that.

Right now his body just refuses to function are in a team. That is something we can overcome given with hard training.

GABLE SAID is been no have been made over the status of freshman Ed DeMoss.

But I'd had been to one think either one will be back this year he said Thomas for now.

But Thomas would, however, take strides and DeMoss will back at the team go with any one this out as

WRESTLING

The Des Moines Register Peach

Des Moines, Iowa, Friday Morning, January 11, 1980

SPORTS

BULLDOGS WIN 116-91 JAM SESSION

Photo By DAVID M. LEWIS

HAWKS LET NO. 3 BUCKS OFF HOOK

11-2 Ohio State burst at end dooms No. 12 Iowa, 77-71

SOPH WATSON, LLOYD DUNK S. ILLINOIS

Duo bags 21, 38 points as Drake slams Salukis

By RON MALY

Welcome to Slam Dunk City Sophomore Tony Watson, starting

Fitzgerald was headed in a new direction now. His goal was altered dramatically; while shedding pounds was his one desire previously, he was now concerned with the pursuit of happiness in a completely different form.

Suddenly, Gable was confronted with a new, stiff and perplexing dilemma. A Hawkeye had quit, and he hadn't seen it coming. There was no easy answer. Gable began to search but found only blanks. The whole wrestling world was watching to see how this "situation" would be handled by the Hawkeye camp. The news media had made a big splash out of Fitzgerald's departure, quoting him as saying the program was too demanding, that it was unrealistic in what it (translated, of course, to mean the coaches) expected out of the wrestlers. The price, he said, was too great.

Concerned as much for the athlete as the program, Gable was not about to give in to the problem. He located Fitz in Austin, Texas, where he was trying to find work. Both were searching for answers, and both knew the answer could only come from one source—Dave Fitzgerald. Like many young people, Fitz needed time to grow up and mature at his own distinctive rate. Wrestling had sped up the maturation process to the point where it was unacceptable. It's a process that has the ability to destroy an individual in one day, or it can mold the national champions of tomorrow. It is, however, a delicate process, with a fine line dividing the possible outcomes.

Gable perceived the situation, and began to understand a new dimension to his job. Sure, he wanted to build great wrestlers, but he also needed to help each of his athletes reach that essential balance between maturity and burnout, between a life of disappointing lessons and a life of accomplishment and fulfillment.

Fitz's life was now out of balance, and had been for some time. He did not know what direction to turn. But like many people and athletes before him, he realized he needed to get away from friends, family, coaches and fans. He needed to take an objective look at his life, and to be honest in his evaluation. Was wrestling really a part of his life, or must he walk away from it? It was no easy decision for a young man in the midst of change.

In retrospect, it seems obvious that Fitz made the right move by moving to Texas and trying his hand at selling insurance and working at manual labor. The realization that life was seldom easy struck him quick and hard, and he knew he did not want to toil and struggle in that fashion the rest of his life. When the season was over, Gable flew to Texas, not with the attitude of a coach but with the concern of a father. Gable did not want to patronize him, but rather to talk with him as a friend. It is this quality about Gable—this concern, which manifests itself only at certain times, but invariably the right one—that makes him special. He wants his athletes to perform well on the mat, but more importantly he wants them to know themselves, to understand what they want in life, and then to act on those goals—goals that he, as a coach, will help them achieve.

He arrived in Austin to discuss the future with Fitz. They worked out together, much in the fashion that old friends will go out on the town; Dave and Dan had their own distinctive bond of friendship. Fitz knew he would return, but he was not certain when. Gable understood. He also knew that a coach can't change an athlete's mind; the athlete has to find his own reason to change.

Fitz had been given the opportunity to think and analyze his situation. He knew manual labor was not for him. He enjoyed challenging himself with difficult management problems, and exploring the vast field of public relations. Deep down inside, Fitz realized he was meant to be around people, to help smooth out conflicts, to be a harmonizer. He returned to Iowa City in May of 1980, his mind firmly set on finishing school, resuming old relationships, and wrestling for the Hawks. He had devised a new plan, one that offered inner peace. He knew businesses would pay for a man who could think, and he vowed to become that type of man.

At the same time, he wanted to enjoy what life had to offer. Though he is hardly the life-of-the-party type of guy, Fitz has a strong, and dry, sense of humor. He was not always easy to read, and I believe that is the way he wanted it. He did not want anyone to figure him out. He sought liberty, and the freedom to live in his own, unique way. It seemed he had found the balance his life was sorely missing before. Now, he had school, friends and wrestling, and his wrestling took on a different meaning. For the first time, he approached wrestling with a serious attitude. Inside, he knew he had to give wrestling one last go. His wrestling days were numbered.

His life took on a new meaning. He enrolled in a military science course, one that I was also in. It gave us the opportunity to share many a story about life in general, and wrestling in particular. And we had a common ground, as I had left the team just one month after Fitz had.

Our common ground was not so much of quitting, but of finding ourselves, and the military science course was a step in the right direction for both of us. It not only offered new companions, but a chance to be a leader, to mature and ultimately to experience something few people do. Leading not only demands that you take the responsibility for your own actions, but for those of others as well, to put the needs of the group before individual needs. This really shook up our world. Though I continued with my military training, Fitz did not, which pleased me because Fitz and I depended on each other during that two-week course, but when it was finished we both had the stability and confidence to make separate choices. He had become a man who could decide what was right for him, and not be swayed by popular demand or other outside forces.

The following year he was back in the groove scholastically, but because he had left school he still had to sit out a year to regain his eligibility. And in the long run, maybe the break was best for him. It gave him the opportunity to sit back, relax and concentrate on school work and relationships with friends.

The following spring, the new Dave Fitzgerald set a goal for himself, to wrestle at 167 for the Hawks. A lot of fans were convinced Gable was the reason Fitz went to 167, but the decision was Fitz's, and his alone. And that's why he could make the sacrifices necessary—because he was doing it for himself, because he wanted to, and for no other reason.

It is my firm opinion that Gable matured greatly, along with Fitz. He learned that athletes need to develop at their own rate, and that they should not be forced to rush nature's process. Also, in a more roundabout fashion, he learned to accept the fact that not all wrestlers, even some of the very best ones, are one hundred percent commited to wrestling, that maybe for many there is something besides wrestling, or even more important than wrestling. Dan had reached a point few coaches reach in such a short time, one that many more will never reach. In competitive athletics, coaches must offer guidance and assistance to the athlete, but only if the athlete is ready and willing to accept it. Too many times, coaches try to live our lives and set our goals. But ultimately the athletes are the people most affected, and must make the decisions that determine the direction their lives will take.

All athletes, I am convinced, know their abilities, their strong points and their shortcomings. A coach can evaluate many things, but there are occasions when he cannot know what is happening inside an athlete. It is up to a coach to relinquish control of an athlete's life when too much control is strangling him.

Gable's coaching philosophy changed after his experience with Fitzgerald. He understood that many of his wrestlers are mature enough and motivated enough to control their own lives, but that some of these same athletes need an opportunity to escape and evaluate their situation and their lives. Dan probably knows what is best for each of his wrestlers, but that is the kind of knowledge many men have to discover for themselves. Many would have to find the answer in a fashion similar to the one Fitz took, and if it meant a departure from wrestling, then so it must. When Fitz returned to school, he did so with Dan Gable in his corner.

Fitz started for Iowa during the 1981-82 season, wrestling for himself and experiencing a new inner peace. He had a good season, compiling a 28-6-1 record and finishing second in the Big Ten and

In deep, Dave Fitzgerald wraps up a foe with a ferocious bear hug. Dave is en route to another crunching pin. Fitzgerald was Big Ten runnerup and an All-American his final season at Iowa. (Photo by Chuck Yesalis).

seventh in the NCAA wrestling meet at Ames. He had a number of big wins for us, and many a time stood with arm raised, an avalanche of cheers enveloping him.

Fitz always knew he could make it in the wrestling world; the real question was whether or not he wanted to. When he discovered his true feelings, he was able to work extra hard and with great satisfaction. He finished his degree in business administration, and returned to the Davenport area, where he has a stable position with a reputable firm. Dave Fitzgerald never won the national tournament, but he scored a much more important victory when he stood his ground in Texas and boldly searched for the meaning of life. It wasn't an easy course he plotted, but it was one of immeasurable rewards.

It was Dan Glenn, a three-time All-American for Iowa, who summed it up best when he said, "Gable doesn't make you win, he makes you want to win for yourself."

In the long run, Fitz became Dan Gable's kind of winner, and Gable became Dave Fitzgerald's kind of coach. And the lessons Fitzgerald learned from Gable extend beyond the confines of a wrestling room.

"The job I have is in a competitive situation," said Fitzgerald two years after wrestling his last match for Iowa. "There aren't the same highs and lows, but my wrestling experience helped a lot. I work twelve hours a day, seven days a week, then get a week off. It's great for a young guy like me.

"The things I went through at Iowa really helped me on this job, no doubt about it," said Fitzgerald. "One thing about Gable—he gets so much out of you. You learn about yourself."

And Gable learned, too.

"I saw him change from when I first met him," said Fitzgerald. "He matured a lot as a coach. He understood we all aren't the same."

Lou Banach

Certainly Ed Banach had a great impact on Dan Gable's education as a coach, but I feel that I, in my own way, also helped Dan grow as a coach. At least, I certainly hope such is the case. It would be a terrific way for me to help pay him back for the way he helped me reach my potential as a wrestler and grow as a person.

I first met Dan in the summer of 1977, when I was a junior in high school and was just starting to travel the year-round wrestling circuit of competition and clinics. That summer was a profitable one for me, as I enjoyed wrestling in the junior nationals even though I failed to place at 191 pounds. Not only was it a great learning experience, but I enjoyed meeting new wrestling friends and talking with the various coaches.

Gable, of course, made quite an impact on me. I wasn't in awe, as I'm not really constructed that way, but I couldn't help pondering what it was that made him so different from all the other coaches. How could this guy bring out the best in mediocre wrestlers while other coaches placed behind him with what were considered to be superior talents? It was an answer that would take me years to discover.

I finished my senior year at Port Jervis, New York, with a 72-3 (52 pins) career record and was recruited by several very good wrestling schools, including Lehigh, Oklahoma State and Iowa. I chose Iowa primarily because Gable was the coach. I considered myself to be semi-motivated towards wrestling and—more importantly—only a mediocre wrestler in terms of talent. Because of that, I believed Gable could bring out the very best I had to offer, and help make me a winner on the highest levels.

Yet when my freshman year began, I found I was not really prepared for wrestling. I was not ready mentally; I felt I needed more time to mature. Fortunately I was red-shirted that season and given the chance to grow and develop. As I watched our varsity athletes in competition, in practice and in conditioning workouts, it was a case of being on the outside looking in. Nothing can compare to what these wrestlers go through; there were two to three straight days of strict dieting, two and sometimes three workouts a day, all just to get rid of that last ounce. I was putting in my time, cutting some weight, hoping to get accustomed to it. But one never really does get used to the pain of weight cutting.

The three Banachs — Steve, Ed and Lou — relax in the wrestling offices at Iowa during the 1979-1980 season. At this point, Ed and Lou were relative unknowns on the national scene, while Steve had just transferred from Clemson University. (Photo courtesy of the *Cedar Rapids Gazette*).

I felt I was starting to mature, and with Bud Palmer graduating, it seemed I would have a spot on the team at 190 pounds for the 1979-80 season. I established my goals for my first year of competition and began the arduous workout routine, lifting weights three times a week, running two or three times a week, practicing my techniques religiously, and wrestling every single day, no matter what mood I was in. I wanted very much to be an Iowa wrestler.

I thought I had achieved my highest goal in just wrestling for Iowa, but I still had a long way to go in maturing and learning about college wrestling. After I defeated Pete Bush 13-3 in wrestle-offs, my position was cemented on the Iowa varsity, and the first few matches were fairly easy. But they suddenly got tougher. I lost a wild 17-15 decision to Lehigh's Colin Kilrain at the Midlands, and stood in the background while my brother Ed won the tournament at 177 pounds. Against Iowa State, I pinned John Forshee to help Iowa to a dramatic come-from-behind 23-17 victory, still, I felt I was losing my interest in wrestling. I had achieved my goal, which was to make the team, and on February 10, 1980, I told Gable I wanted to leave it.

HAWKEYES PIN ISU WRESTLERS, 23-17

ABRACADABRA! 47 POINTS BY LLOYD

'Magic Man' breaks Bird scoring record as Drake soars, 122-76

Photo By BILL NEIBERGALL

IOWA RALLIES ON FALLS BY BANACH TWINS

Cyclones lose final 3 matches, 17-7 lead

Neither Dan or J Robinson, his assistant, were ready to give their approval without a struggle. Dan pressed me for my reasons, and I gave them. I told him that in my viewpoint, wrestling was a business at Iowa, whereas I was only into it for the good times. My grades were faltering as the result of the great amounts of time I had to give the sport, and poor grades were something I was unaccustomed to and disliked. The final point was probably the most important to me—my social life was at a low ebb. My only close contacts were in wrestling circles; wrestling had become my total life and was controlling me.

In my desperation to sort things out, I decided to journey to Texas to visit an old friend. I figured I had to get away from the system, and the bus takes a long time to go anywhere, and gives lots of time to think. But I got off in Oklahoma City. I had made up my mind I was quitting the team, and I flew back to Iowa.

Gable said he could appreciate my feelings and my intentions, but he expressed his concern over quitting anything. "If you quit now," he said, "it will be all that much easier to quit on something else in the future." Now it was my turn to say I could appreciate his point of view, but it would not affect my decision. I had made up my mind to quit, and quit I did. Suddenly, I felt like I was in control of my life for the first time in a long, long while. I felt the freedom to meet new friends and to devote more time to studying. I was able to pull a 3.0 grade point or better every semester after that.

For the first time, Gable realized wrestling was not in my immediate plans, and was not my entire life. He kept a watchful eye on me, and allowed me to continue using the weight facilities and locker-room facilities. He gave me the liberty to run my life. I remember thinking at the time that "someone has finally escaped the ropes of Dan Gable." It was a feeling I welcomed and needed. Deep down, perhaps even Dan felt this way as well.

But the fans were not as understanding as the coach. I had let them down, and let down the Hawks, and that was taboo. Though many fans would stick by my side, understanding the terrific pressures of wrestling at Iowa, most would take a negative approach toward my decision. And I honestly couldn't blame them. I knew I had let many people down, but I felt the need to gain control of my life before it was too late.

But gaining control was no easy chore, I was to discover. I felt like a freshman on the first day of classes, alone and without friends. Yet I had two that I could count on, a woman named Susan, and an army officer. They would prove to be quite helpful in the days and weeks ahead.

Susan became, in fact, my closest confidant and best friend. I talked over my decision with her, and she accepted my arguments. By having someone concur with me, I felt more confident I had done the right thing. Acceptance is what I was searching for, and that was what she gave. She offered honest "gut" feelings. And I also received support from Lt. Colonel Mick Bartelme, the battalion commander of the ROTC unit at the University of Iowa. He is a strong, persuasive man who could sell a refrigerator to an Eskimo. He should have been a statesman.

Money was now uppermost in my mind, as I knew I would have to finance my educaton the next year. ROTC paid one hundred dollars a month, a sum that would be essential. I walked into his office on an April morning and stayed for nearly five hours. He did not question my decision about leaving the wrestling team, but offered me instead the opportunity to join a new team. The commitment he spoke of sounded frightening, however—he was asking for three years of my life after graduation.

As the months passed, I frequently called on the colonel. I wasn't certain if he liked me for who I was, or if I was simply another recruit. We talked about the military, wrestling or anything else that happened to be on my mind. I guess that is why I liked him so much in the beginning; I needed to talk out my innermost problems, and the colonel seemed intently interested. I soon began to feel so comfortable around him that in June I began a course that would give me a real taste of the military. After a while in the program, I felt that I was growing mentally and making lots of new friends, and I joined the army. Initially I was scared to think of the commitment I had made, but I was also satisfied that I was going to have the opportunity to lead people and to take on responsibility.

Many of my friends felt I was just going through another phase, and maybe I was. But it was one that would have a very meaningful impact on my life. I had finally separated myself from wrestling. Financially ROTC would help fill the gap that wrestling left, and that was a comforting feeling.

The colonel had really helped me in straightening out my life, and the opportunities presented by the military changed me. But something strange was happening. By the time my junior year began (it was actually my sophomore year from an athletic eligibility standpoint), I was beginning to really miss the comradeship that I had felt as part of the wrestling team. I contacted Gable and informed him I would like to wrestle again. He advised me to make certain that was what I wanted; if it was, he and J would discuss it and give me an answer.

That night I went home and contemplated my chances of wrestling for Iowa. At 190 pounds, Pete Bush was coming into his own, but I felt I could beat him if I could cut the weight. I was weighing around 220 pounds at the time and felt it would be difficult to trim much of it.

I really began thinking about weight cutting, my old nemesis. Then it struck me, like a bolt from above—that is why I hated wrestling, that was why I quit: I really loved wrestling, but couldn't stand cutting weight.

The only viable solution was to wrestle heavyweight. I could eat, I would be able to keep my social life and I could stay in ROTC. I would be content. I ambled over and told my roommate, former wrestler Mark Mysnyk, that I was wrestling again. He smiled with agreement and acceptance.

The following day, I told Dan I would like to wrestle, but before I had a chance to finish by saying "heavyweight," he said, "You're not wrestling at 190.' He also said I would be happy at heavyweight—that's Dan, always anticipating.

I just smiled and agreed with him. Iowa already had a top-notch heavyweight in Dean Phinney, a 300-pounder who had finished third in the NCAA meet. But he was academically ineligible the first semester and that would give me enough time to show what I could do. As it turned out, Dean would never get his spot back.

And the hard work began, although at Iowa hard work is commonplace. In setting my sights on being the Hawkeye heavyweight for the 1981 season, I started eating mounds of protein to help put on extra weight and complemented the protein with strenuous workouts with barbells—five sets of ten repetitions of such exercises as the bench press, military press, squats and the like.

The weight began piling on, to the point I suddenly understood how pigs feel when farmers pump them full or corn and protein supplements. I was up to 225 pounds at six feet, with a body fat measurement of around seven percent. I resembled a stump; the first part of my heavyweight program was going well.

The next area I worked on—and I mean worked—was running. I never ran in high school, mainly because it wasn't fashionable, or in my training repertoire. Runs of three to four miles every other day soon became a common occurrence in my life. Slowly, but acceptably, I continued the running program, supplementing the distance runs with dashes up the sharp flights of steps at the old Fieldhouse, real "runners" and sprints—things all foreign to the average heavyweight.

With part two well under way, I switched my thoughts to mental toughness. I was a small heavyweight and not the strongest, either, but I felt I was going to be the most determined. I kept telling myself all the running, lifting and technique drilling I was doing would give me the deciding edge in any match. I always tried to do one more rep on weights, or one last sprint, or one more minute of hard wrestling, than I thought I could. And it paid off many times in the months ahead. Many matches I won were won because I never quit mentally, or physically!

Once the season began, I was able to build up my confidence with some fairly light competition. I scored pins against Syracuse and Lehigh, but I began to feel a weakness growing in my right arm. Dan Foster, one of the finest trainers in the nation, gave me a preliminary checkup and discovered I had a pinched nerve in my neck, causing the weakness. Dan felt I should consult a bona fide authority on neck nerves, and Dr. John Albright was called to the observation room. He confirmed my worst fears—that I might never be able to wrestle again. The nerve was weak and further damage could result in paralysis of the right arm.

I wanted so badly to continue wrestling. I faced what I considered to be one of the most difficult decisions of my young life, as tough as the decision of selecting a college is for many others. I felt scared, lonely and empty. Wrestling was suddenly even more important to me than before, but my arm was far more important than any match, tournament or title could ever be. Gable came to me, not out of selfishness but friendship, and explained that he, too, had encountered nerve damage. Doctors had told him to quit wrestling; but he had wanted to be the best, to be an Olympic champion, and so he worked hard to strengthen the muscle column around the neck. First he rested it, then submitted it to punishing conditioning and strengthening exercises. It was a slow process, but it had worked for Gable, and he went on to win the world—twice.

He had been through something I was going through, and he had made it. But he was a machine, programmed for wrestling. I was now at last highly motivated, but the ability to retain my gross motor movements meant a great deal to me. I could not wait much longer; I had to make a decision, one that could affect me for the remainder of my life. Should I quit again, or should I risk it? Maybe the weight program would help, I thought, and I made my decision to continue wrestling.

The decision came just fifteen days before the famous Midlands Tournament, which attracts the nation's top collegiate and postgraduate matmen. It is a meeting place of talent and experience that had seen many NCAA champions fail to win a title. It was probably the grandest test in America for an amateur wrestler, and I wanted to test myself against the nation's best.

My decision firmly made and tucked away, I began lifting again on my atrophied neck. The muscles seemed to understand and respond to the urgency of the situation, and I put one-half inch on it in the time remaining before the meet. I was confident I would be capable of wrestling well, and that the neck and arm would be no handicap.

I drew stiff competition from the beginning, facing NCAA runner-up John Sefter from Penn State in the opening round. Sefter had lost to Oklahoma State's massive Jimmy Jackson, a three-timer, three years before in the NCAA finals, but Gable told me he thought I could beat him. Of course, Dan always believed in his Hawks. It was a hard-fought battle. With me ahead 4-3 going into the final period, I escaped, took John down and finished with a 7-4 victory over the NCAA runnerup.

A newly-acquired confidence surged through me. I needed it, for my next foe was my stiffest challenge ever as an amateur wrestler. I was paired against Wisconsin's Russ Hellickson, who had placed second in the 1976 Olympics in the 220-pound class and was on the 1980 Olympic team which President Carter did not allow to compete. Russ had not lost to an American matman for an unbelievable six years and was a many-time national freestyle champion.

I had worked out with Russ in 1979 at the world training camp in Colorado Springs. To put it bluntly, I could not carry his jock—he was a legend, one of the greatest. He was well conditioned, ox-strong and smart. Gable realized the challenge before me, but told me sternly that Russ was old and someone needed to retire him — someone named Lou Banach. I started to psyche myself up, trying to believe in myself, in my training and my talents. I was young, yes, but I was determined. . . .

As we shook hands before the whistle, I felt privileged but outclassed. Maybe I would lose, but, I told myself, I would be competitive. I would fight like a Spartan until the very last tick of the clock. The match was touch-and-go, but I was ahead 7-5 going into the last, thrill-packed period. With 7,000 fans on their feet, we rushed and pummelled each other early and tried to set up the other for the telling takedown and hopefully the pinning maneuver. Maybe it was Russ' age, or maybe he lacked the fight, that old eye of the tiger; but I ended up winning, 14-6. I had outscored him 7-1 in the final period, scoring on a bear hug!

Russ had another setback in his next match, losing to long and lanky Mike Evans of LSU, 10-2. It was like life, the old fading away and the new coming on to replace it. In wrestling there comes a day when the greats begin to rely on their past experience and knowledge rather than on the long runs, the hours of weight training. There comes a day when even that type of preparation loses out to hunger, the hunger the young competitor brings to the bout.

Maybe, I thought, I am this new, hungry competitor—part of a new breed. I wanted success, but I did not understand at the time the pressure it brought along with it. Success and pressure seem to be roommates.

Success and pressure seem to be roommates in collegiate athletics, but this trio was hungry to take on the wrestling world: From left to right, Lou, Steve and Ed Banach.

In the finals of the Midlands, I ran into the previous year's NCAA heavyweight runner-up, Bruce Baumgartner of Indiana State. We began moving at the whistle, and I was surprised at Bruce's agility and quickness for a man who weighed over 260 pounds. Suddenly I threw him to his back, using my soon-to-be-famous lace leg technique, a move in which I wrap my leg around the opponent's and bear hug him at the same time. It worked perfectly, and I was ahead, 4-0. I tried to end the match and, like a rookie, got overeager. When I cradled Bruce, he slipped through it—mainly because we were perspiring like marathon runners—and managed to maneuver into a pinning position. With two seconds left in the first period, I heard the slap of the mat, by the famous ref Spike Israel.

Dan ran to the edge ot the mat, saying I should hold my head high. He told me he was proud of my herculean efforts, and added that the fans were, too. The encouragement helped, but it was his closing remarks that stuck with me the rest of the season: "Lou, don't be totally satisfied," he said. "You had a storybook tourney, but use it to learn and to better yourself. This is only the beginning."

I tried to be confident with my second-place finish, but I doubted my ability. Then, in the very next meet, I was defeated 18-7 by the same Mike Evans who had beaten Russ. To make matters even worse, I lost the very next match in the most disheartening fashion of all.

With the results of the Iowa-Iowa State meet riding on the outcome of my efforts, and with a full house of 14,000 and a regional television audience looking in, I stormed to a 10-0 lead over 295-pound Dave Osenbaugh at the end of two periods. The Hawks were trailing 19-14, but could win the match if I scored a pin. A superior decision (12 points) would give us a tie.

To this day, I still don't know why I didn't let Osenbaugh to his feet, where I had built the 10-0 lead. Maybe it was the physical exhaustion or the mental strain I was experiencing. Whatever the case, I went instead for my infamous cradle, the same move that had cost me the Baumgartner match. Osenbaugh, who outweighed me by a 75-pound margin, somehow managed to wiggle free as I was pulling him over me, and his weight covered me like a heavy, wet blanket. I could feel his massive, blubbery body on top of me. I felt drained, overheated from work, and incapable of logical thought. Instincts took over. If I had not gotten pinned, I probably would have suffred a heart attack, but my mind wanted to save my body. I relaxed, and the pin was called. It was a pin that came about due to my own foolishness and lack of conditioning.

I lay there on that Cyclone mat for what seemed like a lifetime, as a marathoner collapses after the race. Incapable of thought or movement, I rested on the mat, gasping for oxygen. It slowly filtered down to my empty lungs, and I moved, feeling like a battered warrior retreating from the battlefield. Gable reached for my tired hand. He was sad; the Hawks had lost, and I still had not learned my lesson with the cradle. Still, he was smiling, as a father would after watching his son give it his all in competition and yet still lose. He congratulated me for a valiant effort, even though it ended short of victory—both for me and the team.

A former wrestler at Iowa once told me Dan doesn't really care if you win or lose, but he does care if you give it your very best effort. He understands inexperience, but he won't accept a non-conditioned wrestler or an athlete who doesn't wear the Hawkeye uniform in pride.

That became my slogan for the rest of the year. To give it my best would be all I would ask of myself.

The season turned around for me after that discouraging loss, and I began winning in big fashion. I pinned the previously undefeated Steve "Dr. Death" Williams of Oklahoma in Iowa City. In fact, I never lost again and was seeded second going into the 1981 Big Ten meet. I was on a tear, pinning all three foes and winning the award for the outstanding wrestler. The man I defeated in the finals was Eric Klasson, the defending Big Ten champ who had decisioned me in the dual meet, 4-3. I took an 8-3 lead and then pinned him from our feet with my lace leg maneuver. After the meet, Joe Wells, a former Hawkeye who is assistant coach at Michigan, told a writer that even though he didn't want his man to lose, my going for the pin when I was ahead was what wrestling is all about. But then, I've never been one to sit on a lead.

I had finally won something of significance, and it felt terrific. It was a big boost heading into the NCAA championships in Princeton, New Jersey. Although I was entering my first NCAA meet, I thought I would win because of my superb conditioning and new-found confidence. I was seeded third, and I defeated my first three foes before running into tough Dan Severn, the Arizona State star who had beaten me a year earlier on our western trip, 7-5. This match was a classic, as both of us were small heavyweights, yet quick, agile, quite strong . . . and capable of the big move. And until the last tick, it was a knock-down, drag-out fight. But my conditioning and never-say-die attitude carried me to a 20-10 triumph and there I was, suddenly in the finals and against an old foe, Baumgartner.

Before the match I recalled the words of the world's greatest wrestler, my coach—a coach who understood me. He knew I couldn't enjoy wrestling unless I was out there to have fun. Dan told me, "Just go out there and enjoy yourself. If you do this, then you'll be at the top of the heavyweight class. If not, you'll still have had a hell of a year."

In my mind, though, my Cinderella story wouldn't be complete unless I had avenged the earlier loss to Bruce. I was well prepared, yet he scored a quick takedown for a 2-0 lead. I escaped to make it 2-1, and that's how the period finished. He escaped for a 3-1 lead, but I kept the pressure on with one move on our feet after another, with Bruce countering with some sharp defensive wrestling. Finally Bruce began to tire; at 6-2 and 265 pounds, he couldn't withstand the growling pace of a lighter, better-conditioned athlete. By the close of the second period, he was staggering. He managed a takedown, but I quickly escaped and came back with my own takedown, lifting him high off the mat and depositing him roughly on his stomach. I continued the spartan pace, and he wilted from the lack of oxygen.

I turned him for points, but couldn't hold him on his back for the pin. Bruce gasped for air, and the period ended with me on top, 8-3. The third period was more of the same—Bruce tired and I going for the pin with all I had. I slapped a cradle on him, grabbing one of those trunklike thighs and his gorilla-like neck. I held him for what seemed like an eternity and wondered if he would fight or surrender. I believe he wanted to fight it out, but it was just like my match with Osenbaugh. He was physically exhausted—just like a car that stops when the gas is gone. He stalled and was unable to stop my cradle. I held on like a rock climber afraid to let go or else plummet to his death, and the pin was called. I had come full cycle, from quitting the team a year before to being NCAA heavyweight champion.

The pressure is on as Lou Banach works to turn Bruce Baumgartner for back points at the 1981 NCAA championships at Princeton. Banach led 8-3 in the third period when he cradled Baumgartner and pinned him for the championship. (Photo by Chuck Yesalis).

My junior year was a marked contrast to my sophomore year, when I was struggling to prove myself and gain confidence. This time I was starting out as a marked wrestler, the defending national champion. I became afraid I might lose my crown, but at the same time I was gaining something that would cause problems—vanity. As long as I was considered the best, I thought I would enjoy it.

I began to rely more on my credentials than on the ingredients that had made me a champion. I figured that a champ doesn't need to work out, to lift weights and to run all "that" much. After all, at Iowa all you really had to do was think and believe you were the best, and you would be. It went with the territory.

The only person who really saw the writing on the wall, apparently, was Dan. He knew he had to motivate me and the other wrestlers to lift, run and wrestle, for champions are made on hard, hard work, sweat and determination. He offered to put me through weight workouts at the beginning of the season, and he ran with me, probably to get a fix on my conditioning. I started the season at 230 pounds, but Dan's practices quickly trimmed me down to 215, my fighting weight. I felt confident, healthy and well conditioned. I had not lifted weights at all during the fall, mainly because I wanted to be the best technical wrestler possible and not have to rely on strength. My technique increased, as will anything you practice a thousand times. With my technique honed and my weight low, we embarked on our first road trip.

We opened in Tempe, Arizona, against Bobby Douglas' Sun Devils and were breezing along nicely. I was paired with Mike Severn, Dan's younger brother, and we shook hands and locked up. Suddenly I was on my back, right where Mike had tossed me. "How could this be?" I thought in a panic as the fans screamed wildly. With pure horsepower, I fought off my back as the fans screamed wildly, sort of like a mother who summons up the strength to lift a car to save her child's life; my adrenalin was flowing wildly. I managed to tie the score at 11-11 going into the second period and then came out of my daze, finishing Severn off with a half nelson for a pin in 5:31.

Dan was flushed and emotionless. He told me I had looked physically like a little boy out there. I let his words go in one ear and out the other.

Two days later we were at Cal State Bakersfield, and I was looking for an easy match against the unheralded Roger Herrara, a ruggedly-built man who weighed around 270 pounds. Instead, I barely escaped, and I almost ruined my ankle for good. I hurt it severely, and because I was so weak I could not control the tempo of the match.

Midway through the third period I was leading 12-10, but I was tired, both mentally and physically. My concentration was gone; I did not want to be out there grappling with this brute. I let him go from underneath, sure that I could catch him on my feet. But I was wrong. Roger struck with a quick double, sending 210 pounds flying through the air. We sparred for several seconds again, and then I shot my favorite move, the high crotch. Instead of coming back to my feet, as I should have to correctly finish the move, I stayed on the mat, hanging on to his leg like a dog to a bone. I wouldn't give up, yet each second was draining my strength. Not getting enough oxygen, I became bewildered. I collapsed. Roger drilled me, pushing me over my ankle with the power of a bulldozer. He didn't stop until he received two points and my ankle gave way. Pain shot through my foot; I could feel the blood rushing to the injured area. I wanted to throw in the towel, but if I did, the Hawks would lose, 23-18, and Dan's national champions would be beat. No one understood all of this better than Dan, who came to the side of the mat and verbalized it to me in a manner I could relate to: "Now we can show the place what a national champion is made of," he said, referring to guts, mental toughness and Hawkeye pride. The breather helped me, and I got a chance to gather my wits.

With a minute left, the match resumed. I led, 17-16. It was a barnburner. I struck for a two-point takedown and just as quickly he reversed men, making it 19-18. If Roger had been well coached, he would have led me up for one point, but he rode me for thirty seconds before letting me up with six seconds left. The escape made it 20-18, and that's how it ended. The crowd booed heavily, as it hated the way I had won.

Gable walked to the edge of the blue-trimmed mat and congratulated me, but said I would have to work on my strength, my conditioning, my technique, and . . . well, the list went on and on. The next night,drained emotionally and with my ankle still bothering me, I forfeited. We didn't need the points, anyway, as we defeated Cal Poly, 37-9.

Back in Iowa City I tried to wrestle on the weakened ankle, and it faltered under the slightest pressure. Dan recognized that I needed a rest mentally and physically. When I'm depressed, I lose weight quickly—I don't eat, and I worry like a father whose daughter is on her first date. I don't sleep well until the problem is solved.

The problem was solved temporarily, however. I would skip the Midlands and prepare for the January 9 dual with Iowa State. I had Dan Foster build a special prosthetic device to support my weak ankle. The splint cast offers the mobility of a plaster cast, and after it is taped on it offers the weight of one, too. It also gave me the mental stability and confidence I needed to forge onward.

My training routine switched; there was more emphasis on the lifting, technique work and conditioning. I would pump iron, using heavy weights, for five to six sets of eight reps, then ride the stationary bike for seven minutes (the length of a match) and then go an extra minute of "overtime." J Robinson, the head assistant coach, and Lanny Davidson, one of the graduate assistants, spent an hour or so each night with me working on technique. It was a team effort: Gable, master strategist, devised the routines and the schedule he felt I needed, and the assistants carried through with the diligence of lieutenants.

The ankle was improving, and the swelling was going down, but I couldn't help but wonder if it would be okay in time for the "Donnybrook Series." Mike Chapman, sports editor of *The Cedar Rapids Gazette*, Gable, Robinson and Johnson came up with a name for the Iowa-Iowa State series. They felt if the Oklahoma-Oklahoma State series has its own name (The Bedlam Series), then so should the big bash in Iowa. The *Gazette* provided a ballot, asking readers to pick a name. There were nearly five hundred entries, and they finally settled on The Donnybrook Series.

The first of two donnybrooks took place January 9, and by the time the heavyweight match rolled around, the Hawks had an insurmountable lead, 18-11. My match should have been easy, icing on the cake, no pressure. But someone forgot to tell that to my foe, Wayne Cole, a junior college national runner-up the year before. At six-foot-three and 260 pounds, Wayne resembled a hard-nosed, barrel-chested type of fellow who went looking for scraps and was capable of delivering.

Right from the outset, the match had the fans from both sides leaping to their feet in astonishment. Wayne had a lightning-fast double leg take-down and used it immediately, sending me flying. He easily tossed me around the mat the first several minutes, fashioning a 13-3 lead. I thought my better days were history. I just couldn't get on track. And Wayne had the strength of a blacksmith—at least at first. Then I discovered he also had the conditioning of a heavyweight.

I managed a reversal to cut the margin to 13-5, and suddenly Wayne was dragging, lying exhausted beneath me. The hare had shot out of the starting block in great fashion, but now the tortoise was having his moment. I had drilled bar arms and mat wrestling for two weeks solid, and knew I was about to be given the chance to work what I had practiced. It was my chance, maybe my only chance, and the bar arm worked like a magic wand. Wayne rolled to his back without much resistance and without a great deal of effort on my part. It is amazing how technique works! The fall came quickly, and the Hawks took the meet by the score of 24-11.

Once again I was a winner. Dan and I had the attitude that I should take one match at a time, resting for the easy matches and preparing carefully for the big ones. My ankle was improving, and I felt confident it would be able to withstand the tests ahead. But I was hit with another calamity; just as the ankle was shaping up, I was struck by a severe bruise and strain in my right shoulder. It was more than just a physical setback, too; this injury really bothered me mentally, as I had just begun to feel reassured aout my wrestling. It was back to the drawing board—and to the stationary bike in the weight room.

We were preparing for our western trip, and I was down mentally. At Oklahoma State I would go against Mitch Shelton, a giant who tipped the scales at close to the 400-pound mark. How could I compete with him when I had a bad ankle and a sore shoulder? My attitude was low; I wanted to finish the trip and the season; I wanted to segregate myself, mentally and physically. As it turned out, it was the worst trip of my Hawkeye career. I lost to Shelton at Oklahoma State, 5-2, and finished with a tie at Oklahoma. Steve Williams, called "Dr. Death" because he is so big and looks like the professional-wrestling types you see on TV, had wanted revenge for my pinning him in Iowa City the year before. But we finished in a 2-2 tie.

Dejection set in; I was upset with my performances. But Dan seemed pleased. He always seems so positive; he can see good in everything. If a glass was half empty, he would see it as half full. Positive! He told me that at least I got two good, hard matches in, and I was healthy. We could use that as a foundation for the future.

I worked hard on my ankle and shoulder, and the combination of hard work and time seemed to heal my battered body. I felt healthy for the second donnybrook with Iowa State. Even though I had pinned Cole in the first go-around, I felt he had humiliated me in the early going, and I was hungry for revenge. I took a 19-7 lead on Wayne this time before pinning him.

Once again, his heavyweight conditioning let him down when the going got tough.

I had high expectations about the tournament season fast approaching, but they were dashed when I reinjured my shoulder just one day before the Big Ten meet in Michigan. Once again, though, Gable came to my aid; he stripped away most of the pressure I was feeling by saying I only needed to qualify for the nationals, and not to risk further injury. He told me I could beat any of these heavyweights with two bad ankles and two bad shoulders. I wish I could have been so confident.

As it was, each match was a war. I needed at least forty minutes to loosen up the shoulder and the ankle, and I felt like a piece of battered meat as my teammates and coaches pulled and tugged at me, trying to get me prepared. Somehow, probably because Gable was on my side, I made it to the finals. But I didn't want to wrestle at that point, and Dan didn't want me to, I found out later. We failed to communicate, however, and I was soundly beaten by Eric Klasson of Michigan, a man I had defeated two weeks earlier, 16-6, and had pinned in the Big Ten finals the year before. This time, his 11-7 victory not only earned him the Big Ten title but the outstanding wrestler award, as well.

I was a tired and sore warrior, physically beaten. My first words to Dan were "I wish I hadn't wrestled." He replied that he wished he hadn't wrestled me. We burst out laughing like two school kids who had just heard their first dirty joke.

For the next ten days I did no wrestling, not once. Dan learned that the rest helped me more mentally than physically, so he agreed to let me take it easy. I ran a lot, though, carrying buddies on my back while running the stairs, and I rode the bike. But I could not lift weights, as the pain in my shoulder was too severe. One week before the tourney, Gable, Foster and Dr. Albright discussed my situation and decided I should have an anti-inflammatory steriod to relieve the shoulder stress. It would relieve the pain and help bring back lost strength. The decision was left up to me.

I took six pills, and almost overnight I felt stronger. When I moved the shoulder, it felt better, but it sounded like pieces of bone were being rubbed together. I knew the rubbing, use and lifting were all detrimental, but I only had one more week to go, and I could take that.

When I hit the scales at 206 pounds at the NCAA meet, I was the lightest heavyweight in the field. Each match chipped away at my confidence. I defeated George Fears of Navy, 18-14, and scored a dramatic fall over 410-pound Tab Thacker of North Carolina State in the first period. Then I lost my first match ever in the NCAA tournament when Williams of Oklahoma defeated me, 7-4. In two days, I had taken a beating; I could no longer move my shoulder. My arm just hung at my side, paralyzed with pain. I had failed. I was no longer a national champion. I could not muster up enough guts to wrestle the final day. If you think the wrestling in the NCAA tourney is demanding . . . well, let me tell you the wrestlebacks are twice as tough, mostly because wrestlers find it very difficult to motivate themselves after semifinal losses. To say I was heartbroken would be an understatement. I wanted to be the best again.

So I made up my mind I would go down fighting.

When the wrestleoffs started, I was there. I defeated Mike Holcomb of Miami (Ohio), 6-2, then found myself facing my old nemesis, ISU's Cole. The match was to decide who would be third and fourth in the NCAA meet. It turned out to be, according to most accounts, one of the most exciting matches in the entire tourney. I could not begin to tell you how the points were scored; I just know I won, 11-10. In the finals that night, two men I had pinned the year before battled for the title, with Bruce Baumgartner decisioning Steve Williams.

Two vastly different types of heavyweights battle for position at the 1982 NCAA tournament in Ames. Lou Banach, weighing around 206 pounds, scored a first-period pin over 410-pound Tab Thacker of North Carolina State. (Photo by Chuck Yesalis).

It was over. I had finished third in the NCAA, despite a number of problems. It was a tourney that treated me roughly, but made me grow up, and in more ways than one. I realized that I was lucky, but also that hard work is what makes winners, and that lame wrestlers don't last long. I promised myself I would never have another season like the one I had just completed. Either I would work hard, lift, run, practice technique very diligently, or I would hand in my shoes. Being around Gable I had learned not to settle for second best and not to live on yesterday's headlines.

Iowa pins down 5th straight title

By Mike Chapman and Brian Chapman
Gazette sportswriters

AMES — It was a big night for little Barry Davis in Hilton Coliseum.

Iowa's indefatigable 118-pounder won his first NCAA championship by defeating Iowa State's Kevin Darkus, 7-5, Saturday night. The victory:

(1) Clinched the team title for Iowa, giving the Hawkeyes their fifth straight and making Dan Gable the first mat coach to ever win five in a row.

(2) Gave Davis a single-season record of 46 wins (against one loss), the most in Iowa history.

(3) Made Davis the first NCAA wrestling champion ever from the Cedar Rapids area.

The Hawks had an NCAA-record 131 3/4 points, while Iowa State finished second and Oklahoma third. The Cyclones scored 111 points, but had just one champion in 150-pounder Nate Carr. Oklahoma had 109 points, and four champions.

Oklahoma State was fourth with 71 3/4 points, followed by North Carolina with 47 and Nebraska with 40 1/4. Northern Iowa was 10th with 26 points.

And Oklahoma also had the meet's outstanding wrestler in Mark Schultz. The muscular junior outscored Iowa's two-time national champ Ed Banach in the 177-pound finals, 16-8, in one of the truly fine matches of the last decade.

Davis didn't remain the solitary champion from the Metro area for long. Jimmy Zalesky, like Davis only a sophomore, won the 158-pound crown by dominating Perry Shea of California State-Bakersfield, 10-3. Missouri earlier Zalesky's older brother Lennie faltered in his 142-pound match with Oklahoma's Andre Metzger. Metzger's 9-6 win handed him his second NCAA crown in as many years. Metzger defeated Zalesky in the finals of the NCAAs one year ago.

This time Zalesky took a 4-2 lead at the end of the first period with two takedowns against two escapes. He went ahead 5-2 on an escape to open the second period, but then the roof caved in.

Metzger, underhooking each of Zalesky's arms and bulling him around the mat, picked up a stall call to make it 5-3. The Sooner escaped quickly in the third period and then picked up another point on a debatable stalling call, tying it 5-5. With just one minute left in the match, Zalesky, trying frantically for a takedown, grabbed hold of Metzger's uniform and was assessed a two-point penalty.

Metzger scored a counter takedown and Zalesky escaped for the final 9-6 count. Metzger's only offensive points came on the late takedown.

Davis and the Zaleskys are from Cedar Rapids Prairie High School, and Jimmy became the second Prairie Hawk alum to win a national title when he socked Shea with three takedowns, one near fall and one point riding time (3:13) for his margin of victory. Shea, who had gained the finals with an upset of defending two-time NCAA champion Ricky Stewart of Oklahoma State, had beaten Zalesky 8-2 in a dual meet in December.

"The first time I think it was just a fluke, because I think I outwrestled him and he caught me with just one move," said Zalesky. "Coach Gable told me I had to be on him all the time. That's what I did. I kept the pressure on him."

Zalesky, who gave up just one takedown in his five matches in the tournament, said this is the best he has ever wrestled.

"I wrestled every match really intense," he said.

The record crowd of 14,204 (73,576 for all sessions) was stunned by the developments at 177.

Banach went ahead on a takedown and nearfall and an escape against a reverse for a 5-7 lead. But Schultz came on like gangbusters, winning a battle of bear hugs for a takedown and near fall and 6-5 lead as the first period ended. It was 10-8 late in the match when Schultz countered Banach's takedown attempt with a takedown and near fall to ice the victory.

Schultz, a former gymnast, did a standing back flip after the match and was greeted by his brother Dave. Dave was also a champ, outlasting Oklahoma State's Mike ● Please turn to page 2C: NCAA

Iowa Hawkeye wrestling coach Dan Gable intensely studies action at the NCAA tournament in Ames

That spring found me resting, eating and drinking my beer, but all in moderation. I thought about hanging it all up, but I was not yet number one. Because of that, I decided I had to continue with my senior season.

When school started in the fall of my senior year, I was caught off guard. Could it really be, I asked, that I am really a senior, in my last year of college? Only yesterday I had been a freshman. How the years had flown.

My shoulder was still sore, with what my doctor called a resorption. I called it a pain in the ass. I could not lift; the joint was just too weak. All the bruises caused inflammation, which was literally eating my shoulder away. It really needed rest for a year, but that would wipe out my final season. I received cortisone injections, followed by immobilizaton for over a week. Suddenly my shoulder was no longer snapping like a broken tree limb. I was healing.

With wrestling still two months away, I began light lifting—just ten to twenty pounds. Slowly the poundages increased and I was ready to step on the mat with healed ankle and shoulder. I wanted to become one of "Gable's boys." (Rumor has it that Dan calls us his boys because he has no sons, just three lovely little daughters, at home. To him his wrestlers are his boys.)

I felt strong, quick as a cat and full of energy. My shape was good, but I needed to work on my technique a great deal. That was not something that came totally naturally to me, as it did with Mike DeAnna, our four-time Big Ten champion at 167 pounds. I increased my workouts, the running mileage, and felt on top of my game. In the wrestleoffs I faced Steve Wilbur, a good, tough wrestler from Indianola, Iowa. Steve has the potential to be one of the best, if he puts in the necessary time. I defeated him 16-5 and by pin, and for the fourth straight year I would be a starter for the Hawkeyes, the greatest team in wrestling.

It seemed to be going easily, too easily. I racked up ten straight wins, and it seemed almost like taking candy from a baby. But the Oklahoma State Cowboys came storming into Iowa City the night of

A pensive Lou Banach sits on the sidelines with former Iowa star Randy Lewis, sizing up his next opponent. Both Lou and Randy won two NCAA championships for the Hawkeyes.

December 18, 1982, intent upon upsetting the top-ranked, high-flying Hawks. My foe was Shelton, the near-400-pounder who had decisioned me the previous season in Stillwater, 5-2. Before the match I was nervous, something different for me. I had visions of myself getting pinned, and I don't know why. But I couldn't jar that thought from my mind. In wrestling, if you think you are going to get beat, you will.

I thought Mitch would pin me, and I found myself getting very tense, unsure of my conditioning and technique. I didn't know if even my strength would help me against this giant. As it turned out, the only thing that would have helped me that particular night would have been a crane. Eddie had just pinned Karl Lynes, leaving us ahead by 24-21. I tried to throw Mitch right away, deceiving myself into believing I could toss a 400-pounder in that way. Locked chest to chest, we teetered and came down hard, with me underneath. I had lost by a fall in just one minute and thirty-five seconds, the Hawks lost 27-24, and I had been defeated for the second time by Shelton.

Now I was faced with even a bigger problem: How could I win nationals? Shelton was there in my path, a huge, unyielding roadblock. I felt my interest in wrestling waning. I didn't want to continue. I retreated to the security of my old girlfriend and her family, for rest and relaxation—which were really the last things I needed. With a woman's instinct, she told me I needed to wrestle, to work out... and to overcome that defeat.

We ran together—distance, stairs and sprints—and I felt my conditioning improving, but not to where it should be, which I knew deep down inside. After the runs, my heart wasn't pounding with the sound of work in it, it just sounded mildly taxed.

I wanted to wrestle, but I didn't want to lose again. It seemed the only way to regain my confidence was to enter the Midlands Tournament. I had not actually wrestled in a week, but I had to try and recapture a winning attitude. There in Evanston I won my first two matches, lost by criteria to Dan Severn, the former Arizona State star I had beaten in the NCAA meet my sophomore year, and then won my next three, finishing fourth. I didn't win the Midlands, but I placed ahead of Shelton. In turn I defeated Matt Ghaffari of Cleveland State, 12-4, the man who had ousted Mitch. My fire was rekindled; I knew I could win the nationals with a little help from other wrestlers.

The season began to take off again. I pinned all my opponents in the Big Ten meet to recapture the crown I had lost the year before. Assistant coach Mark Johnson became my shadow. He put me through strenuous lifting and running sessions. A member of the 1980 Olympic team in Greco-Roman, Mark is probably the strongest wrestler in the world. He has placed very high in top physique meets and was once featured in a national magazine (*Strength & Health*) for curling 250 pounds ten times. Mark was watching me closely, because he knew it would be difficult for me to quit with someone monitoring me intensely, and he made the sweat roll off my brow.

At the NCAA meet in Oklahoma City Myriad Convention Center, I was wrestling very well. In my first three matches, I had two pins and a 26-10 decision. My "friends" didn't knock off Shelton, however, and we were dead on a collision course. It was now up to me, and my conditioning had never been better—and neither had Dan Gable's coaching. He scouted Mitch at the Big Eight tourney against Cole, a match Wayne won, 11-2. Gable told me not to wrestle him, but to push him and play cat and mouse to tire him out. I was not to shoot on him, not to try a single hold, just shove him around and tire him. I was ready to listen to Gable. Wrestling Mitch my way had failed. Maybe coaching would do the trick.

In my estimation, it was an uneventful, boring match. But Dan's strategy paid big dividends as I won, 3-1. I scored on a reversal and riding time, while Shelton only picked up an escape. As the seconds ticked off in the last minute, I felt as if I had 400 pounds of pressure lifted off me. Because I had beaten Cole so many times before, I felt certain I was going to realize my goal of being national champ again.

Now for the second time in three years, I found myself in the finals against Cole, who was much improved from the previous season and was having a terrific tournament. Wayne was handling good heavyweights with ease, and had won seven straight matches since I pinned him in the second dual meet. He started fast against me, as always, scoring with a deep double-leg takedown. But then he began to wilt, and I pinned him in two minutes and fifty-eight seconds, taking him straight to his back with a bear hug.

The college career was over. Eddie and I had left our friends and home in Port Jervis five years earlier, heading to Iowa City and our destiny. We were raw, young kids, looking to find a spot to grow and to develop, not only as athletes, but as human beings. Ed finished his career as the pinningest and winningest wrestler in Iowa history. He became the sixth man in Big Ten history to win four league championships, and the first three-time NCAA champion in University of Iowa history. He had wrestled twenty matches in the NCAA tourney, and had won all but one, scoring more NCAA tourney points than any wrestler in history.

And I had done all right, too. I had two Big Ten titles to my credit, and two NCAA championships. I was almost always outweighed in my matches, but I felt I more than made up for it with Hawkeye attitude. I wrestled in three NCAA tournaments, and came out with a 15-1 record. Not bad for a guy who had crawled on a bus three years earlier and headed for Texas, determined to put wrestling behind.

Although I did grow as a person and athlete, I know Dan Gable

Wayne Cole of Iowa State University is sent flying by Iowa's Lou Banach. The two tangled on six occasions during college, with Lou winning each match, including the finals of the NCAA championships in 1983. (Photo by Chuck Yesalis).

The Banach era at Iowa bows out as Lou wins his second NCAA championship and is greeted by Ed, at the conclusion of the 1983 NCAA tournament in Oklahoma City. In the preceding match, Ed claimed his third NCAA title. (Photo courtesy of *The Predicament*).

grew right along with me. That is why he is such a fantastic coach—he is open to growth, giving it a chance to work its wonders. He accepted me as an individual, someone who simply could not live wrestling day in and day out.

Maybe I was that new breed of athlete that Eddie was, and that Barry would become. And that Dave was, and that Rico would be. I cared for wrestling, academics and social growth equally. But the biggest lesson of all was that I learned—and I mean learned, sometimes the hard way—to listen to my coach. Maybe Dan, the other coaches and some of the wrestlers thought at times that I was given preferential treatment, but I don't view it that way at all. I was given individual treatment, and a large dose of understanding. Dan adapted to my style and I adapted to his—and we met halfway.

There is always a bottom line in success stories, and this one is no different. It is this: the Iowa way is the Dan Gable way, and the Dan Gable way, actually, is simple: work hard, harder than the opponent will be willing to, and train yourself to be a winner. Discipline and tolerance are the two attributes that must go hand in hand in today's college athletic system, and Iowa wrestling has both, in large degrees.

That's why they are the best today. And maybe the best collegiate athletic team ever assembled.

Barry Davis

We affectionately call him "Sparrow Hawk." He's a Hawk of the noblest kind, but he's also a sparrow in size. He's also a different type of athlete—one who has yearned for victories, labored hour after hour, and never settled for second best—all in a fashion that sets him apart from most good wrestlers I have known.

At Prairie High School in Cedar Rapids, Iowa, Davis fought for recognition in a school that also boasted the Zalesky brothers, Lennie and Jimmy. Davis' go-go style caught on big with the fans, and he battled his way to three state titles with an indefatigable approach to wrestling. He was like a runaway windmill, asking no quarter and giving none. Though many schools courted him, he knew deep inside he was born to be a Hawkeye, and to wrestle for Dan Gable.

"I came to Iowa because I knew Iowa was the place where I could become the best wrestler I could possibly make of myself," said Barry, reflecting on his decision to attend Iowa.

Sparrow is always a pleasure to be around. He never questioned the workouts the Iowa staff offered, or Gable's philosophy. With the obedience of a foot soldier in a Roman Legion, Barry accepted and progressed.

Watching this young, hungry and intense athlete develop was fascinating. He had the stubbornness of a mule, the quickness of a cat and the slyness of a fox. He ran, lifted and wrestled as if there was no tomorrow; and maybe to Barry, there wasn't. Perhaps that is why he struggled so hard for success. For Barry there is no better time than today to make a name for yourself. Day by day, we watched him develop into a superb, never-say-die opponent who would punish wrestlers three years his senior.

Davis could be considered a "coach's dream"; in fact, there were those who were calling him the next Dan Gable. Even as a freshman, he was mature enough to run his own life. In wrestling, he was a real leader; he was one of the foremost Hawks in terms of conditioning, technique drills and intensity.

Yet beneath that composed exterior there was a problem waiting to surface. It would take a while, but surface it would—when least expected.

Davis won the Big Ten title at 118 as a freshman, and placed seventh in the NCAA Championships at Princeton in 1981. He finished the season with a 35-6 record, and left behind a ton of trimmed-off weight. While other wrestlers were preparing for the victory party at Princeton, Davis went back to his room and continued to train, subjecting himself to a strenuous series of pushups, situps and drills. He worked for over thirty minutes, sweating away the disappointment of a seventh-place finish.

"Today I train. Next year in Ames I'll be on top," he said solemnly.

Davis would finish on top in Ames, but not before going through an emotional roller-coaster ride that would shake up his teammates, his many fans and even Gable. The episode would attract nationwide attention, even in places not given to covering wrestling. *Sports Illustrated* and *The Sporting News* would relate the Davis story, as would all corners of the state of Iowa.

Davis began the 1981-82 season in typical Davis fashion, rolling over foe after foe. All the time he was paying an immense price, struggling to keep his weight at the 118-pound limit. Even the best machine will fatigue itself with overuse, however, and Davis overworked his body. He was spending one to two hours each day,

A common scene at Iowa in the early 1980s was that of Barry Davis pinning a foe. At the end of his junior year, Davis was a two-time NCAA champion at two different weights — 118 and 126.

lifting weights and working on technique, then two to three hours wrestling in the afternoon, followed by watching tapes of opponents. He was also working hard on his studies, and concentrating on controlling the urge to eat, the ongoing battle all wrestlers under the heavyweight classificaton must wage.

To the rest of us, it appeared as though Barry was starting to be just like Gable, and Gable appeared to love it. But trouble was brewing.

"Coaches can get too caught up in wanting the athlete to win, without noticing the signs of boredom, fatigue and burnout," said Davis two years later. He was hovering near the burnout point; it would take very little to push him over the edge. There is a tendency for coaches who get too close to an athlete to overlook any weakness and Barry, like the rest of us, had one. It was deeply submerged, but it finally pushed to the surface. It was a weakness which, when recognized and controlled, would make Barry even more of a wrestler and more of a man.

In the wee hours of the morning of March 1, 1982, Davis found himself all alone in the Iowa wrestling room. Though he never complained, he had been fighting a fierce battle with his weight. This morning he stripped, slipped on his cold rubber sweat suit, hopped on the stationary bike and began pedaling furiously.

After just several minutes, he stopped pedaling. He was alone with his pain and his thoughts. Every athlete, whether he plays baseball, football or wrestling, needs to be surrounded by teammates who can offer encouragement and support. On this particular morning, Barry could not have been more alone.

Sweat to a wrestler is like gold to a commodities dealer. When a wrestler is trying to shed the last couple of pounds, it is precious. Barry could not even break a sweat. Without a coach or teammate to offer support, he surrendered mentally. He changed back to his street attire, slowly, tears dripping from bloodshot eyes. Weight cutting had had its day.

At 5:30 a.m., an hour later, the rest of the Hawkeyes filed into the room, preparing to depart for the Big Ten Championships in Ann Arbor, Michigan. We wandered in listlessly to pick up wrestling shoes, check our weight and dab water on our parched tongues. We gathered around a bench as Gable informally took role.

Dave Fitzgerald, our 167-pounder, broke the mood as he called out to Gable, rather nervously, "Gabes, I think you should read this."

Fitz had discovered a letter left by Davis, and he handed it to the shocked coach. The letter said that Barry had quit the team. It expressed his confidence the team could win the league title and the nationals without him, and wished us luck.

Gable quickly gained his composure and said he had planned it all because he wanted us to win the nationals with just a nine-man squad. But the team was hit hard; every wrestler on the team was close to the never-say-die, 118-pound dynamo. He was always cheerful and outgong, a great leadoff man for all of us. We missed him, and we were perplexed. We couldn't understand what had happened to Barry to cause him to leave. I wondered why none of us had seen it coming.

I had a lump in my throat. Suddenly, there was no catalyst to spark my fire. I felt lonely, because if one Hawk was missing, we all suffered emotionally. The Hawks were a tight-knit group, maybe not overtly, but through that competitive spirit that Hawkeyes are known for. Now, our chain of unity was broken. We needed to mend it.

Matt Egeland, a young and upcoming Hawk, was called to fill in the void. Matt responded to the call and slowly crawled into his cold and clammy sweat suit to begin shedding the vital pounds. Gable and his assistants began to bombard Egeland with the positive thinking so crucial to a Hawkeye. The process to weld back the chain was set in motion. But Davis was a hardened, forged and seasoned player, whereas Matt was as yet rough and untempered.

Gable rounded up a posse to begin the search for Davis.

Matt Egeland, a former state champion from Des Moines Dowling, was thrust into a starter's role three times during the 1981-82 season, and almost took Barry Davis' spot in the Big Ten meet when Davis left the team briefly. Here, Egeland receives some top advice after a disheartening setback. (Photo courtesy of the *Cedar Rapids Gazette*).

Steve Wilbur, the backup heavyweight and Barry's roommate, tried to offer all the information he could summon. It wasn't hard to figure that food would be uppermost on Barry's mind, and the hunt began by hitting all the convenience food stops in Iowa City.

Around 6:00 a.m., Gable pulled into a Hy-Vee food store parking lot to use the phone to call more wrestlers into the manhunt. Wilbur, accompanying Gable, peered into the store and spotted a sad, lean and tired young man standing in the checkout line. In disbelief Wilbur took a second look and then nudged his coach, who was on the phone.

"I think I see Barry," said Wilbur, pointing into the store. Gable was off like a flash, displaying the agility of an O.J. Simpson as he bolted into the store. Gable confronted Barry, who was holding a bag of doughnuts. A moment passed as they stood without speaking. Then the bag dropped to the floor and Dan approached his wrestler, dropping an arm around his shoulder.

Gable asked what had happened, and Barry explained he had broken under the pressure of cutting weight for months on end—and particularly this morning at 4:00 a.m., alone with his thoughts in the dark and quiet wrestling room. Gable understood, and vowed that Barry would never have to face that situation alone again. Gable offered to be his partner, to see him through the loneliest part of being a top-flight wrestler. It was a process the coach would repeat one year later with Ed Banach.

The team had flown on ahead, so Davis and Gable caught the next flight to Chicago, where they had a layover. They worked out together, almost like a father and son, running, talking and sweating together. Barry learned once and for all that he was the member of a team on which even the coach participated, and that he would be asked to do nothing even the coach would not do.

Barry was seven pounds overweight when the plane touched down in Chicago, and two pounds—a tough two pounds—over when it took back off. Already he was feeling dizzy, a dryness in his mouth and a weakness in his stomach, all common occurrences among wrestlers.

When the plane landed in Ann Arbor, the Hawks were asleep in their hotel rooms with the knowledge Barry was on his way. Word had been sent,and we knew the chain would be strong once again.

The Big Ten tournament was a painful one, but satisfying for the Hawks. We crowned seven champs—and Barry Davis was one of them, winning his second straight at 118 pounds. Two of the Hawks who came up short were Dave Fitzgerald and I. Dave lost to Dave Ruckman of Ohio State, and I was decisioned 11-7 by an old nemesis, long and lean Eric Klasson of Michigan, the same fellow I had pinned in the Big Ten title match the year before. We were second, but second is not a place to hang your hat on in the Hawkeye wrestling room.

The Hawkeyes pulled together in the following ten days, and Barry, in particular, came alive again. He defeated five straight foes to win his first NCAA title, and finished the season with a 46-1 record, setting an Iowa record for most wins in a single season. He had weathered the storm and become a stronger wrestler. More importantly, he became a stronger man, for he had learned how to deal with adversity without buckling under it. It had taken a giant of a man to quit, to admit things were not going right and that a change of direction was needed, but it took an even bigger man to come back with the style and grace Barry exhibited.

Barry Davis, one of the most aggressive wrestlers in Iowa History, works over a foe during the 1981-82 dual meet season. Davis set a Hawkeye season record with 46 wins (and a 46-1 record) in 1981-82.

But the Barry Davis story doesn't stop there in Ames, with his first NCAA title tucked safely away. People say winning comes easily for a Hawkeye. I'll agree it comes "easy" but only because we make it so hard on ourselves in the practice room. Technique drilling, running the stairs, lifting weights, reviewing film, dieting, sweating and just plain hard wrestling—it all takes place each and every day of practice during the regular season. We earn the right to stand at the top.

And Sparrow didn't burn out again. He continued his training after the season, and earned a spot as the alternate on the world team at 125.5 pounds, losing a close match to John Azevedo, the former NCAA champion from California State at Bakersfield.

Barry entered the 1982-83 season with a fresh outlook, and in a new weight class. He was going to move up to 126 pounds, and set his goals to not only win the nationals there, but to make the Pan-American Games and world teams, as well. With the consistency of a Swiss watch, he trained day and night, buoyed in part by the experience the year before that had been tranformed from a negative influence to a positive one. Undefeated going into Christmas break, he suffered one of his rare losses at the Midlands Tourney, dropping a 6-2 decision in the semi-finals, to his old foe, Joe McFarland of Michigan, then coming back to dump Ed Pigeon of Hofstra for third place.

Disappointed at placing third, even in a tournament as tough as the Midlands, Davis intensified his workouts. He would lead the morning runs by 100 yards, and the tough stairs run by twenty stairs. He would wrestle nonstop for one hour solid, take a one-minute water break, and be at it again for another hour. None of his partners could keep the furious pace, and Gable rotated three or four fresh wrestlers in on him constantly. Then Barry would tire physically, but never mentally.

He was hungry and fresh when the Big Ten tournament opened in 1983 in Iowa City in the new 18-million-dollar Carver-Hawkeye Arena. Davis breezed to his third straight Big Ten championship and captured his second NCAA title, this time at 126, in Oklahoma City. Just three weeks after his NCAA triumph, he was in his hometown of Cedar Rapids as part of an American team taking on the Soviet Union. At the pre-game meal, he and his Soviet foe, Andre Fartzev, sparred in fun, but the Soviet backed away after a few seconds, grinning but breathing hard. Barry read the message correctly: He knew the Soviet couldn't keep his pace in the match if the Hawkeye would really open up. The next night, before nearly 6,000 wildly screaming fans, Davis worked his opponent from the other side of the world into a state of exhaustion and took a brilliant 8-5 victory. Barry ran around in a circle and rammed his fist into the air as he received a tumultuous standing ovation from his hometown fans. He had come a long way from the cold and lonely wrestling room where he had quit the Iowa team in frustration and pain.

But Davis wasn't the only one to benefit from the experience in March of '82. It was another step in the education of the coach, and Gable proved once again his extraordinary ability to grow with each experience and to turn even a negative force into a positive one.

Communication was at a minimum between Gable and many of his wrestlers at the time Davis broke away. Like their coach, many of the Iowa wrestlers are quiet by nature, preferring to keep their innermost thoughts to themselves rather than burden another with their problems. Coaches need to be aware of this tendency and slowly, throughout the season, develop a rapport with the athletes and get to know them as individuals.

And we all learned that even the greatest of athletes—even a wrestler of Barry Davis' stature—needs to be watched, studied and helped at crucial times. Davis, like Dave Fitzgerald before him and Ed Banach and Rico after him, would prove to be just one of the many testimonies to Gable's greatness as a coach.

Davis' development as a wrestler continues. In September of 1983 he was crowned king of the entire Western Hemisphere, winning the gold medal in the 125-pound class at the Pan-American Games in Caracas, Venezuela. He made the world team the following month, but lost his first two matches in Kiev, Soviet Union. Even that momentary setback did not deter him.

"It was a mental thing," said Barry, back in Iowa City. "I had never been overseas before, or in a world tournament. I think I got caught up in it all a bit too much. But it was a great learning experience. It's a whole other world, another big step up. I'll be ready for it next time."

Davis has also matured in his approach to training. Though he still trains with a devotion few can match, he has learned when to slack off when the pressure becomes overwhelming.

When I observe Barry, now, I see an inner peace. He still loves to work and to achieve his goals, and he still enjoys his wrestling immensely. But he is secure enough to take time off if the circumstances dictate that he do so. He has matured from the shy, young matman who startled the Prairie High School fans with his amazing performances to the world-tested athlete who very well may end up with an Olympic gold medal, either in 1984 or 1988.

If he does, much of the credit will go to his coaches, and to Gable in particular. "There's only one way to describe Coach Gable," said Barry two years after quitting the team that lonely morning," and that is 'The Master.' " To me, and many others, Barry Davis is one of the finest examples of what wrestling, Hawkeye style, is all about.

Tim Riley

Experiences, positive or negative, have the capacity to broaden an athlete into a more complete and understanding individual. This certainly proved to be true with Dan Gable on a number of instances.

The education of Gable as a coach would not be complete without the inclusion of the story of an athlete who, heading into his final season in 1983-84, had not yet made it all the way to the top in the world of big-time wrestling. Tim Riley represents the type of wrestler — like Davis, Banach and Rico Chiapparelli — who gained a multitude of valuable experiences in high school and summer camps, yet Riley for some reason failed to scale the utmost heights at Iowa. He developed a non-flashy wrestling style, but still became a cornerstone in the Hawkeye program. More importantly, perhaps, was the challenge he threw at Gable—the challenge of helping Riley become, despite the obstacles he presented, a national champion.

Born and raised in Iowa City, Tim had the opportunity to observe the Iowa program firsthand for many years before becoming a part of it. Though he seemed destined to become a Hawkeye star, stardom never developed. Instead, he became in wrestling, in a loose sort of way, what Rodney Dangerfield is in show business—a man searching for respect. On the other hand, Dangerfield, who is constantly in motion—twitching and jerking his overweight body like a puppet dancing on a string—is the antithesis of Riley, who never seems able to shift into a gear higher than first. In the view of most fans, Riley seems forever moving at a pace less than frantic, and he has developed a style that contrasts sharply with the brilliance exhibited by a Randy Lewis or a Rico Chiapparelli.

"I'm not sure why I don't wrestle at a quicker pace," said Tim in 1984, slouched on a chair in my living room. "Maybe it's because I'm bored, or the season is too long. Or maybe it's my shoulder that holds me back [it has been dislocated five times]. Or maybe it's my lack of total love for the sport. . . ."

Although Dangerfield has developed a style which is a gimmick to market his product—which is, of course, entertainment—Tim's style is not a gimmick. A gimmick is only successful if it attracts a crowd; Tim's style, for the most part does not fall into that category. Yet Riley is quick to admit he wants respect in the wrestling world. And the surest way to gain respect, as well as fulfillment, is to win the national championship. It is a goal he ponders frequently.

Tim Riley was a two-time state champion from City High of Iowa City before joining the Hawkeye fold. At Iowa, Riley became a three-time All-American wrestler, twice at 118 pounds and once at 126 pounds.

"Sure, I would like to be a national champ," he says without the trace of a smile. "I've put over a decade into wrestling so far. I would be a fool if that wasn't my goal."

But attaining his goal will not be child's play for Riley, for he has experienced the setbacks that go hand in hand with college wrestling: There has been the loneliness of defeat, the bland agony of countless workouts, the hell of cutting weight. Loneliness and agony are all more than just casual visitors in the wrestling rooms of America, wherever they may be located. Yet there was a day when Tim Riley rose above all the setbacks, and stood at the very top of the ladder.

Slowly, as is his style, Riley fashioned himself into one of the best high school wrestlers in the Midwest. Together he and coach Clyde Bean laid the groundwork for the years at Iowa in the days at City High School. The work was climaxed by three trips to the Iowa State High School Wrestling Tournament in Des Moines. His sophomore season, Tim finished third, losing in an early round to senior Jim Gibbons, who was destined to become an NCAA champion for Iowa State University in 1981. But placing third provided invaluable learning tools for Riley, and gave him a confidence that would carry him to state titles as a junior and senior. In the summer of 1979 Riley went one giant step farther and captured the 132-pound championship at USWF Junior National Wrestling Tourney. It was the same meet that featured such standout grapplers as Ed Banach, Mike DeAnna, Randy Lewis and Jeff Kerber in other years. Riding high, Riley attracted scholarship offers from several of the nation's powers, including Iowa and Iowa State. But the decision on where to attend college, considered by psychologists to be one of the three biggest decisions a person will ever make in his or her life (the other two being the selection of an occupation and a marriage partner), was no tough task for Riley.

"I've lived in Iowa City all my life," he said several years after making his choice. "I like the team, the people, the whole atmosphere. It wasn't a hard choice."

In the fall of 1979, however, the easy choice suddenly developed into a hard reality. Thrust into the Iowa wrestling room with the likes of All-Americans Randy Lewis, Dan Glenn and Lennie Zalesky, Riley was on the receiving end of many lessons. He found improvement slow in coming, and his confidence waning. He rationalized that "guys in college are tougher, stronger and better technicians: In high school I was a physically punishing wrestler, but now I need to put in more time." He needed to work harder in all the various elements that comprise a successful wrestler.

The slow climb to the top had begun for Tim. The three-time Mississippi Valley Conference and two-time state champion was experiencing the incredible power of the Iowa wrestling program—up close and personally. Then came one of the worst blows of his athletic career: Battling for a varsity spot, he was defeated by another freshman, Jeff Kerber, the Emmetsburg four-time state champ with the flashy 126-0 high school record. Riley finished with a respectable 11-7 varsity mark as a freshman, plus the bitter memory of not earning the right to compete in either the Big Ten or national meet. And there remained the haunting loss to Kerber.

"That Kerber loss really affected me," said Riley five years later. "I still remember it, and I guess I always will."

Disgruntled and disillusioned just one season after being at the top of the high school scene, the young Hawkeye took time to rethink and evaluate his freshman campaign. Concluding that he needed more consistency in three basic areas—conditioning, technique and mental preparation—he zeroed in on them, and on the NCAA tournament in Princeton, New Jersey, his sophomore year:

Riley made great strides his second season, even if he did not attain his ultimate goal. He closed out the year with a 27-9-0 record at 126 pounds, placed fourth in the Big Ten and seventh in the NCAA (All-American status for seventh and eighth place had been awarded in 1980 by the NCAA rules committee). He had not gone all the way to the top, but he had come closer—much closer, in fact—to his long-range goal.

Riley had completed two rough and demanding years at Iowa, and it was time for a break, at least in the thinking of Gable and Robinson. They decided Riley needed to allow time for growth, both mentally and physically, and they provided him the time to reorganize by putting him on a red-shirt season (taking a year off from the athletic competition). It was an approach welcomed by Riley.

"If Gable thinks all I need is to work hard at wrestling and it'll happen—I'll get tougher physically and mentally—then it's worth a try," Riley felt at the time. Red-shirting is a process that can work one of two ways on a wrestler: It can provide a respite from the rigors of competition, and allow him to refresh himself, rekindle the flame for the sport and become very productive (like Darryl Burley of Lehigh in 1982); or it can sometimes take the athlete too far from the competitive arena and ruin his mental outlook. John Bowlsby, who finished third at heavyweight for Iowa as a freshman in 1975, red-shirted the following year with an injury, and never matched his freshman placing again. He later claimed he never was really able to get into the groove again after red-shirting.

Riley began his sabbatical with trips to Cuba and Australia, and began training with the national freestyle team in the summer of 1982. For him, the year off would prove to be a year well spent.

"My redshirt year was most enjoyable," he recounted two years later. "I got a chance to travel, wrestle in foreign lands and to gain confidence in my wrestling."

Perhaps most important of all in Riley's case, it took him out of the pressure situation of competing for the Hawkeye team. Though he was still wrestling and working out, he carried a different viewpoint and perspective. It was, all in all, a good year for Tim Riley.

But when the 1982-83 season approached, Riley was greeted with a distressing piece of information. Barry Davis, NCAA champion at 118 pounds, had wrestled his last bout at 118. He was growing, and was moving up to 126. Davis' decision would herald the beginning of what would prove to be a roller-coaster season for Riley, one of ups and downs in terms of injuries, confidence and fortunes.

Riley forfeited the opportunity for tryout matches with Davis at 126 and began the descent to 118 pounds, a weight he had not seen for years. It would call for the cutting of an inordinate amount of weight, and the price would be high in many respects. During the summer of 1982, he pared down to a slender 130 pounds in preparation for the upcoming season. The loss of some twelve pounds under his normal weight presented Tim another problem: His regular attire was now loose, and Tim began to look sloppy and slovenly in his appearance. He subscribed, if at times unwillingly, to Gable's philosophy of regulating weight over a long period of time. Day by day he watched the weight slip off slowly as he controlled his caloric intake, so by the time nationals arrived he would not have to face a staggering weight loss.

As the months passed, he slowly lost the weight—and muscle mass and strength, strength so essential to a wrestler during the final month of the season. But while his strength was diminishing, his conditioning was improving; the more weight he lost, the more refined his system became, with no extra bulk to burn up oxygen. He was paying the ultimate price of college wrestling with the very sweat of his brow.

Early in the season, Tim found the matches rough and mentally disturbing—and so did Gable. At Michigan State, Riley had a difficult time with the weight and it affected his performance. He looked sluggish and lethargic, to the point where Gable yelled out at the referee to call him for stalling. Gable hoped the move would motivate his 118-pounder to take the offensive, but it did not. Nor would it have solved the underlying problem. Tim's body was weak and lacked the necessary nutrition and time to recover from weigh-in. And his spirit, once so strong, had grown weak, too.

Eventually, Riley was disqualified from the Michigan State match for passivity. According to Gable, it's embarrassing for an Iowa wrestler to hold back. "People fear Iowa," Gable said afterward, "and I can't let an opponent make a mockery of one of my guys. I don't

Struggles on the mat are only half the battle for a wrestler like Tim Riley. The smallest Hawkeye for two of his last three seasons, Tim had to struggle valiantly to keep his weight down to 118 pounds.

want them to lose their motivation and concentration." At any rate, Gable's psychological maneuverings were lost on Riley at that point.

"I think he's crazy and a lunatic at times," said Riley when assessing the situation two years later. "But other times," he concluded, "I think he's the greatest."

The weight-cutting problems were far from over, and they resurfaced again prior to matches with Oklahoma State's Randy Willingham and Iowa State's John Thorn. Gable intervened, but with the care and patience of a father trying to find the solution to a son's problem. He analyzed the situation as one where Riley had spent most of his time working on cutting weight and honing his techniques, but had neglected conditioning, which was one of Gable's fortes.

The cure, in Gable's mind, was to install Riley on the three-day routine. Tim, along with Ed Banach and Harlan Kistler, would undergo workouts at 4:30 in the morning, then again at 8:30 a.m. under the watchful eye of either Robinson or Johnson, and finally terminate the day with a hard wrestling practice at 4:00 p.m. with the team. It was not an experience that Tim reflects fondly upon.

"Two-a-day practices is a good coaching philosophy," he said, "and to survive is a compliment. But three a day is next to madness. It had to work because, for sure, no one else was even thinking about it, let alone doing it. I hated every minute of it, but I believed they would give me the deciding edge in my matches."

Although Riley's final statement holds true for most wrestlers, it didn't work that way for Tim. He had stirred up Gable's interest in his lack of motivation and action, and Gable responded with six weeks of three-a-day workouts to try and jolt him into action.

The shock worked for some time. Riley won 15 of his last 19 matches, and walked off with the Big Ten championship by soundly defeating Robin Morris of Wisconsin in the finals. Fittingly, the tourney was held in Iowa City, and the hometown crowd was treated to the sight of Riley wrestling at his best. Riley entered the NCAA meet with high expectations.

But the first round brought the ceiling tumbling down on him. Battling with Thorn, a wrestler he had decisioned rather handily earlier, he lost a boring match with little action. Thoroughly depressed, Riley was ready to toss in the towel and end his mat career.

"The loss to Thorn disgusted me," said Riley. "If all that work didn't help, then it was time to give up wrestling. I was finished. I wanted to quit."

Suddenly Riley received an encouraging boost from an unexpected source. In order for Riley to enter the NCAA wrestlebacks, Thorn needed to gain the semifinals by defeating top-seed Willingham, who had beaten him by an overwhelming margin in the Big Eight finals. And that's just what Thorn did, turning in an inspired performance for a shocking upset. Riley was back in the tournament.

His long-range conditioning program stepped back into the picture, too. Wrestling with a new determination and enthusiasm, Riley won five matches, including one over Willingham, and finished fifth at 118 pounds. It was his conditioning, in the long run, that had made the difference.

Tim Riley is on top of his game and in control as he takes an opponent to the mat during the 1983-84 season. (Photo by Chuck Yesalis).

Riley entered his final season of competition in 1983-84 equipped with the knowledge that he could defeat the best—men like Willingham—on any given day. But he was also aware, painfully, of the limitations he had to cope with. In the final evaluation Tim appears to be an athlete who grows mentally tired from the long and constant pressures of his sport, and consequently has matches where he is only "going through the motions." Even Gable, the master motivator, is not capable of drawing a wrestler out of that mental cocoon for every single match of a long season. Riley, for whatever reason, is an athlete who will experience periodic ups and downs. And he has learned to face the dilemma head-on.

"I know I can't be on top of my game, or up mentally, all the time," he said during the 1984 season, "so my goal is to start out slowly in August and keep my life intact. That means including school, parties and friends. By the time January comes, I've learned to discard a few of the distractions, and by the time the Big Tens and nationals come, I've put the partying and the good times on the shelf, and readied myself for the last five to six weeks.

"I wish I could tell you why I can't be consistent in my style; I want to be a reliable wrestler, but for some unknown reason that escapes me, at least for the present.

"I'm willing to meet Dan, J and Mark halfway in my commitment, but that's all I can do. If they give me a fair shake, I'll give them one. Dan will meet someone halfway, but I know he's not in the missionary business, pulling people out of the gutters and making them champs. They have to meet him halfway, too."

The coaches do more than meet an athlete halfway, however. They are usually on the scene at seven in the morning, and remain till seven at night, sometimes longer. Work is the mainstay of the Iowa program, and that's where the coaches—Dan, J and Mark—lead by example. Riley proved beyond a doubt he was willing to meet the coaches halfway and pay the torturous price of three-a-day workouts, yet he has been denied the national championship. Maybe, however, he has gained something more important than the label "national champion." Maybe he has discovered not all of one's goals and dreams come true, and the glory is in the chase and the commitment as much as in the reward.

Perhaps Gable has discovered some basic truths, as well, through the trials and tribulations of Tim Riley.

"Gable would like to have all of his athletes in one mold, under one hat, but he also knows that would not be reality," said Mike DeAnna, the four-time Big Ten champ who joined the Iowa staff on a part-time basis before the start of the 1983-84 season. "And it would not be fair to the athlete to expect the same results from all of them. As a coach, he needs to figure out how to bring out the best in each athlete. That is Dan's job, and he is still learning."

What Gable has learned is that Riley often performed to the limits of his ability and missed winning a national championship. But by giving the utmost, Riley gained a new stature. He discovered he had the aility to work incredibly hard—harder than he would have ever imagined possible five years earlier as a high school student—and that life is full of ups and downs, all of which balance out over a long period of time. Winning a wrestling match is not the only measure of a wrestler's worth, even at Iowa.

Tim Riley, in my book, is a winner—an athlete who paid the price and who stands at the top of the ladder, holding his head high. And Dan Gable is a better man for having coached him.

Rico Chiapparelli

Rico Chiapparelli: It's an interesting name, which conjures up interesting images in Iowa wrestling circles. There's the big, toothy grin, the shock of black, curly hair, the gangling physique, the exciting, do-or-die style of wrestling, the pins. But for the Iowa wrestling staff of coaches, the name also meant confusion and sometimes trouble.

Rico's story begins in Baltimore, Maryland, where he won three state wrestling titles, compiling a sparkling 119-4-1 record with an amazing 94 pins. He sounded like another Randy Lewis, who came out of the bleakness of South Dakota with three state championships and an 89-0 record his last three years, which included 83 pins. Maybe Rico wasn't blessed with the pure talents of Randy or Mike DeAnna, but he had a unique style that caught the eye of Dan Gable.

My first acquaintance with Rico left me bewildered. He was clumsy, unorthodox and unpredictable, not only in the wrestling room but in everyday life. Motivation, self drive and discipline are all qualities Rico has, but they are not always obvious. Even a wise man wouldn't necessarily have bet that Rico had them, and certainly a few Hawkeye fans would not have. But he does indeed have those characteristics in large measures. In fact, it was his motivaton and determination that landed him in Iowa City at the Iowa Intensive Camp—not once, but four times! It's a camp for serious wrestlers only, and most are delighted to have survived it once. It took Chiapparelli four times to satisfy the hunger that drove him.

At first glance you might figure Rico to be a basketball player rather than a wrestler. Tall and slender, he does not carry a great deal of muscle. But when he first walked into the Iowa Intensive Camp, it was as though he owned it. One would have thought he was the principal stock holder, and that attitude made it easy for a lot of wrestlers to take him with a grain of salt—and to underestimate him.

Even the camp counselors regarded Rico too lightly and began to lose interest in him almost immediately. We assessed him quickly as just a young kid going through a stage. We figured if we paid him scant attention and gave him little time, he would leave us alone, an

Rico Chiapparelli came to Iowa with very impressive credentials. He won three state high school championships in Maryland and compiled a 119-4-1 record, which included a tremendous 94 pins.

out-of-sight, out-of-mind arrangement. I guess, truthfully, that most of us felt Rico was too far out of the picture, to really be worth spending much time with. We were judging the book by its cover, which was to be our mistake.

But what's that saying—you can't keep a good man down? Rico kept showing up; four straight summers he was at the camp. He became "one of the boys." He is very perceptive as an athlete. He studied his technique and practiced it with diligence and determination. Though it would never come easy for Rico, he stayed with it, working hard. Rico, an intelligent kid (he had been accepted at Harvard), understood strengths and weaknesses, and what to do about them. He knew that, given his long and gangly physique, he was going to have to rely on technique rather than power to bring him through. I believe he developed as a wrestler so quickly and efficiently because he analyzed and understood his physical talents and limitations, and knew that to be successful he was going to have to play the numbers game, to know when to roll or to elevate a foe going to his own back. It was a game of high risks and high odds.

Technique became the backbone of his wrestling. And at the high school level that is a highly marketable and attractive quality for coaches scouring the nation looking for raw talent to develop. As a junior in high school, Rico was his own man, toying with and eventually destroying most of his opponents. Sure, it would often look as though he were about to lose, but suddenly he would arch, turn like a contortionist, elevate himself with a leg, scramble off his own back, squirm like an eel, and then force the foe onto his back where, weary and emotionally drained, he would surrender the pin in another wild and woolly Chiapparelli victory. But while the coaches were smiling and the fans were screaming, Rico showed no emotion or sign of excitement, for it had all come so easily. Rico had developed the style carefully and skillfully, and he fully expected the results that came.

Chiapparelli spent his senior year at Blair Prep School in New Jersey, transferring from Mt. St. Joseph High School, which he had attended as a junior. Blair was an institution that had been attended by such wrestling greats as Mike Frick, two-time NCAA champion for Lehigh, and the Lieberman brothers, Mike and Mark, also NCAA champs at Lehigh. At Blair, the competition was keen and intense. On the wrestling schedule were perennial prep wrestling powers from the states of New York, New Jersey and Pennsylvania, and there was also occasion to compete against college matmen in various wrestling tournaments. With the competition, Rico gained valuable experience and matured, all the while facing many of the same problems that college freshmen go through—being away from home and friends, balancing a budget, and the like.

When Rico showed up in Iowa City the following year on a

wrestling scholarship, there was even more adjusting to do. Right from the first day of school, he and Dan Gable never seemed to understand each other. Both were strong in convictions, confident in who they were and what they wanted to be. Both wanted the very best—Gable for his athletes, and Rico for himself. Rico wanted the national title as a freshman, something very few first-year collegiate wrestlers can even dream about, let alone approach. At Iowa during the Gable era, only Lewis and DeAnna really came close as first-year freshmen, Randy taking second at 126 pounds in 1978, and DeAnna finishing third at 167 pounds in 1976. Rico's wrestling was very important to him, but so were his schooling, his new-found friends and the college environment. To me, Rico is an observer of life, one who sits back and quietly learns from others. Nothing fancy, but effective.

Rico's freshman year was a real learning experience for him, as he swayed back and forth in evaluating what was and was not important to him. One day it was wrestling, the next day it was friends, the next day school. Gable had a difficult time trying to understand his freshman from Maryland. Meanwhile, through all the changing, Rico was trying to test his coach, to see just how much power Dan had— and perhaps to see if his new coach would accept him for what and who he was.

Gable liked Rico as a person, and cared about his growth at Iowa. He helped Rico through the rough academic times by arranging tutoring from Dr. Mark Mysnyk. Of course, it wasn't that Rico was incapable of doing the work; he just wanted to see if Gable would help. Rico treated it like a game, a game to test the commitment of his coach to the athlete. It was a game Rico enjoyed, but Gable did not.

Gable quickly saw through it all and lost patience with it, at the same time becoming very concerned about his new Hawk. There was the chance Rico would play himself right out of the lineup, and maybe out of school as well. Chiapparelli had a solid core, but he still had the problems nearly all freshmen have....searching for an identity and trying to find security in a new, often trying environment, and trying to fit into an athletic squad of unparalleled success.

In retrospect, perhaps one could charge that the reason Rico wrestled so uniquely and strangely is that he wanted notoriety, to attract a certain degree of attention. At Iowa attention is spread evenly over all the starters, and maybe Rico needed to elevate himself somehow. Whatever the case, by midseason, Rico was struggling and Gable was struggling with him. Gable had to determine what size role he should attempt to fill; should he step in and try to help as much as possible, or leave the decision to Rico? If he helped, would history repeat itself, and would he encounter the same resistance he found in Fitzgerald and the Banachs, or would he find the acceptance he had come across with Barry Davis? It was no easy decision, but he knew if he did not take some form of action, Rico would not be in the national tournament come March.

Gable's decision was made for him while watching Chiapparelli in the first Iowa-Iowa State dual meet. He was facing Jim Lord, a former three-time state champion from Lisbon who was actually little more than a 142-pounder, but had jumped to 167 in order to make the Cyclone lineup. From the start, Rico seemed to be in a daze, and he lost, 10-6. But it was the manner in which he lost that infuriated Gable. With seconds left in the match, the Iowa freshman calmly turned his back on Lord and began walking away, as though he was scarcely concerned with what had transpired. Afterwards, Gable was stern when addressing the press: "Chiapparelli will change his attitude," said Gable, "or he has wrestled his last match as a Hawkeye."

The decision had been made; Gable would not stand idly by and watch Chiapparelli take the wrong turns. Gable wasn't about to change Rico's style of wrestling, as he believes in improving a person's style rather than changing it. He wants a wrestler to improve on his strong points, and eliminate his weaknesses through sheer hard work, concentration and growth. Gable felt Chiapparelli's style was okay, but that he needed more strength in order to complete his moves. He needed strength to be more competitive on the college level, and Rico was put on a weightlifting program. The program may have been too late to have much effect on the season, but it would lay the groundwork for the years to come.

In the Big Ten meet, hosted by the Hawks in the brand new 15,000-seat Carver-Hawkeye Sports Arena, Rico was up and down. While nine Hawkeyes took league crowns and Iowa shattered the all-time scoring record with 200 points. Chiapparelli had to settle for fourth place. But it was an exciting fourth place. Time and again, he brought the appreciative wrestling crowd of around 10,000 roaring to its feet with his wild, innovative style. On several instances, the fans responded with standing ovations. Along the way, he managed to pin his 19th foe, which was a new Iowa pinning record for one season, breaking the old record set by heavyweight John Bowlsby.

The fourth-place finish, the wild card berth, allowed Chiapparelli to gain the NCAA tourney in Oklahoma City. Rico worked hard in the room before the NCAA meet, and Gable stayed in the distance, monitoring him but allowing him to feel he was in charge. Rico started out the national meet by defeating seventh-seeded Colin Grissom, Yale but then we ran into second-seeded John Reich of Navy. It was a rough-and-tumble affair, and Rico gave a good account of himself before bowing, 12-5. Chiapparelli fell short of his goal; not only was he not a national champion as a freshman, but he had failed to place.

It was an up-and-down freshman season for Rico Chiapparelli in 1982-83. He finished the season with a 25-10 overall record and set a record for pins by a freshman at Iowa with 19.

Yet the season was a success for the Maryland flash. Besides the pinning record, he had compiled 25 wins for an overall record of 25-10. The following season he was red-shirted and continued to work with weights, trying to build the strength that, coupled with his uncanny moves, should take him to the very summit of the collegiate wrestling world. And he helped Gable progress even further in his development as a coach. Even more than ever, it was impressed on Dan the need to treat each athlete as an individual, to understand that each wrestler has his unique chemistry and makeup, and each dances to the beat of a different drummer. I think Dan also learned that sometimes even a coach has to stand back out of the way of a neophyte athlete, and let him suffer and go through growing pains— although of course, he needs to step in too. Each wrestler, and each person, needs to find his own path through life. Guidance is helpful, but it can also be counterproductive at the wrong times.

The paths of Dan and Rico are destined to cross continually over the next several years as both work on the goals they have individually and collectively set. They will work side by side not only as coach and pupil, but as friends. No longer is the successful coach functioning solely as one who directs or instructs, callous and removed in attitude; instead he offers the guidance and direction that come from one who really cares, a friend and comrade in arms. Gable is a master at assessing a person's cares, and setting him on the proper path to correct them. He has proven that time after time after time. And Rico helped Dan to grasp even firmer that unique ability he has, and to employ it at just the right time and place. Understanding and changing Rico for the better can only make Dan Gable a much better coach. Together Dan and Rico could prove to be an unbeatable combination.

3

THE HAWKEYE RECIPE

J Robinson:

The "Secret" Is Plain Hard Work

It is September 1972. Richard Milhous Nixon is President of the United States. The war in Vietnam is slowly winding to a halt . . . . and Dan Gable and J Robinson have just finished competing in the 1972 Olympics in Munich, Germany. Gable has won the gold medal in the 149.5-pound class by blanking all foreign competitors. J has failed to place in the Greco-Roman competition after finishing fourth in the 1970 World Games and fifth in the 1971 World Games. Weeks later, Iowa's head wrestling coach, Gary Kurdelmeier, hires Gable as his new assistant, and Olympic teammate (and roommate) Robinson ventures to Iowa City to work as a graduate assistant coach, hoping to learn and grab some of the magic of Dan Gable, master of the sport.

The time is February 1984, twelve years later. The years since Munich have proven extremely fruitful to both Gable and Robinson, who have jointly fashioned one of the most powerful wrestling programs·since the reign of Oklahoma State University in the late 1930s and '40s. The chemistry of the Gable-Robinson tandem seemed bound for glory right from the beginning, for they are born of the same mold—one of dedication, discipline and commitment.

"We at Iowa, whether secretaries, assistant coaches or athletes, learn to work hard and make a firm commitment," said Robinson in 1984. "Dan, Mark and I just direct their talent and energy in one common direction: the NCAA title."

He minces no words when describing Iowa's objective: "Our goal at Iowa is to be the best wrestling team, year-in and year-out, in the nation," said Robinson. "You have to set your priorities high, and then work to attain them. It makes very little sense to settle for less than first after you put all that time in practice."

And Robinson speaks from experience, as he is no stranger to second, or even last, place.

J Robinson gets a lift from team captains Jim Zalesky (left) and Pete Bush prior to the start of the 1983-84 season.

"All my life has been a growing experience," he said. "I've known what it feels like to finish last in a tournament, to finish in the middle of the pack, and to finish first. Believe me when I say I know what it feels like; but through all my wrestling, I've learned what it takes to be a winner, to be successful. And this is what I want to impart to my kids at Iowa."

What J has learned came from his time spent at Boy Scout camp in sunny San Diego, California, and it gathered momentum during his years as a captain in the Army. And he also learned a great deal about work, and the work ethic, by observing his father.

"As a youngster, I watched my dad work," said Robinson, reflecting on the days of his youth. "He loved it. I didn't understand that notion until years later when I started wrestling and went through Ranger school. Through work I realized you can find happiness—but you have to give one hundred percent to your God-given talented area. Work is like brushing your teeth—it becomes a cleansing, refreshing habit. And that's what I try to instill in the kids who venture to my 28-day wrestling camp, or my guys at Iowa.

Coaches J Robinson (left) and Dan Gable provide vocal support for one of their wrestlers during the 1982-83 season. (Photo by Chuck Yesalis).

"I don't choose to be a common man. I want to be better tomorrow than today. And through a commitment to work and discipline, but mostly hard work, I'll be a little more content, and a little different from the average guy," he added.

Once Robinson turns to the subject of work, he can talk virtually nonstop. It's one of his true passions in life, and he makes no bones about it.

"That is the main problem with people, and the world in general: Everyone has forgot how to work for a living. At my intensive camp, I look at kids like a blank sheet of paper, with no writing or distortion. Either I can imprint on them my work ethic, something that they will use and carry with them through life, or I can choose to let them loaf. Both are learned traits, but the former is much more useful and healthy for life.

Robinson's philosophy expresses the essence of the Iowa program. Each new recruit MUST learn early to love work if he wants to be a national champion. The athletes at Iowa, maintains Robinson, must learn to pay the price. In the beginning the amount of work seems inordinately high in terms of hours spent practicing, but once they accept the work habit, then the commitment becomes easier to make and accept. For some, it takes one or two years to adapt to that ethic and lifestyle, but success will come in the long run to those who pay the price.

"At least the percentages are with those who do," said Robinson.

Robinson, of course, is asking nothing from athletes that he himself has not done. After giving over twenty years of his life to wrestling, after fourteen operations—seven on the knees, three on shoulders, and an assortment of others—Robinson knows he has paid the price of competitive athletics. But in addition to paying the price, he has perfected the formula, a formula that not only prepares you for wrestling, but for life as well.

"Through wrestling, through the hard work and the sweat, through the victories and the defeats, we learn a great deal about ourselves," claimed Robinson. "Wrestling shows you your limits, your weaknesses, your strengths; and ultimately, you grow because of what it shows you."

Robinson conveys the feeling that he cares dearly about his athletes. Fatherly-like talks and big brother-like chats with him reveal his personal interest in the individual, his work, and his life.

"At Oklahoma State [where J wrestled collegiately], I didn't have too many people who took an interest in me, or cared for me," he said candidly. "Because of that, I never really grew as a wrestler or enjoyed myself. After winning my first national tournament in 1970, I called my high school coach, Ned Blass [who was a two-time NCAA champion for Oklahoma State] because I wanted to share the excitement I felt with someone who cared. At Iowa, I try to make the kids understand that I care for them. I try to get close, within professional limits, so that the kids understand that I care for them.

"By showing you care, that becomes a positive action with that athlete. If you care and believe in an athlete, then he will start believing in himself, too."

Each fall J invites a psychologist from Chicago to come in and work with the team, to help the wrestlers learn how to believe in themselves. Behavior scientist B.F. Skinner would probably take easily to J's way of thinking: "Sometimes you have to over-kill—you just have to keep ramming it home that what you're telling them is for the best. You just have to make them learn a positive response and habit. Some guys like Barry Davis and Jim Zalesky learn that right away. Some are stubborn, like the Banachs, and compromise with the coaches a little, and even a little with themselves. And some— well, they just never catch on and leave Iowa."

Old-fashioned, archaic and outdated may be the way some people choose to label J's feelings, but they are nonetheless effective. J may indeed be out of the past. He still believes there is a God, and that family and country are important.

"If you care and believe in an athlete, then he will start believing in himself, too," is the philosophy J Robinson brought to Iowa. Above, Robinson sends Tim Riley out to battle. (Photo by John McIvor).

"Whatever happened to taking pride in your work?" he asked. "What happened to serving your country, and what has happened to the work ethic? We are in a society that constantly wants more, but isn't willing to work for it," he said, a trace of sadness developing in his voice.

J believes in the simple things in life—things that are snickered at by city folk," but which are in style with those who want to earn their place in life through plain hard work.

"I guess that's why I like working on my farm," said Robinson, referring to his acreage about ten miles north of Iowa City. "People might call me old-fashioned, a cowboy; but in being a cowboy I'm totally in touch with hard work. I'm in touch with nature. I don't need a lot of expensive things around me. I have my family, animals and hard work. It may be a simple life, but it is effective and it is where I find my happiness."

To Robinson, simplicity is the "trick" to life—just living as simply as possible and doing your best at whatever you choose to do. The "secret" to his success is so extremely simple.

And this is the essence of Iowa's success, too. There are no real "secrets," no lucky people, but simply those who set high standards and work on the basics: technique, lifting, conditioning and mental toughness, and who try to get the very most out of their God-given talents.

It's the same message one hears in the adage a friend of mine likes: "I believe in luck—and the harder I work the luckier I get." Truer words were never spoken, it seems to me.

And assuredly, J Robinson is one of these "lucky" people. He is an example of commitment and dedicaton that tenderfoot recruits would do well to study and to learn from.

"When a recruit comes to Iowa, I'm going to do my best to make him feel at home and comfortable," said Robinson. "And, I'm going to meet him halfway in his quest to become a national champion. If he is willing to make the effort, I'll be more than willing to accommodate him.

That's a philosophy shared by the entire Iowa staff.

In the fall of 1978, when Ed and I were freshmen, J would meet us at 5 a.m. (that's in the morning, guys) and drive to Cedar Rapids, nearly thirty miles away, in order for us to use Nautilus equipment, which the University of Iowa did not have available at the time. For three straight months, every Monday, Wednesday and Friday, we journeyed to Cedar Rapids so the Banachs could improve their strength and muscular endurance. Robinson proved he was more than willing to meet us halfway in our quest to become national champions.

In February of 1984, following a shocking 24-6 loss to Oklahoma State in Stillwater, the Iowa wrestlers discovered once again the depths of Robinson's commitment to the team. The day after the loss, the team began working out three times a day each Monday, Wednesday and Friday, with sessions at 7 a.m., 4 p.m. and again later in the evening.

"In talking with Dan and the team, we felt we needed something extra to get us over the hump and give us a fine edge for the nationals," said Robinson, who was serving as interim coach while Gable concentrated on working with the United States Olympic team. At Iowa, success comes wrapped in a total effort, borne by all.

It is 1984—George Orwell's year. It is a year of coined phrases such as "newspeak," "doublethink" and "Big Brother." It is a year that has also produced a few more gray hairs on Iowa's interim coach, and has caused J to contemplate more than ever his future in wrestling.

"I'm getting old," said the veteran of hundreds of matches and more than a dozen operations, a man who has travelled the world as a wrestler and a coach. "In another four years I'll probably retire. I can barely wrestle with the guys. It will be time to move out of coaching when I no longer can."

For Robinson, wrestling is more than coaching from the side of a mat; it's teaching by example, as he did as a platoon leader in Vietnam, and as he did in his early days as a graduate assistant at Iowa. It's setting goals and working as hard as is humanly possible to achieve them. It is an honesty with yourself that cannot, and should not, be denied.

That is J Robinson's message, and Iowa's. It is also life's. Either you play by the rules—the rules of hard work, long hours, commitment, discipline and caring—or you drift aimlessly in life and accept mediocrity.

Soon it will be 1985 . . . and 1986. . . . whose year will that be? Will it be yours?

Mark Johnson:

Lending Strength to the Total Program

Many humid Midwestern summers ago, Mark Johnson, like many thousands of youngsters searching for a sports hero, chose Dan Gable. And it was only natural that this native of Illinois sought Gable's autograph—an autograph which to a wrestling fan is on the same level as Babe Ruth's would be to a baseball follower, or Arnold Schwarzenegger's would be to a bodybuilding enthusiast.

Today Mark Johnson finds himself in the somewhat ironic position of working for the wrestling legend whose autograph he pursued. It's a twist of fate that Johnson fondly reflects upon.

"I knew Iowa was searching for an assistant coach [in the summer of 1982], but I had no idea that Dan wanted me," said Johnson during the 1983-84 season, after nearly a year and a half on the job. "Heck, a few years back I wanted his autograph, and now I'm working for him. I consider it an honor and a compliment for Dan to hire me."

At Iowa there is the need to recruit athletes with the winning attitude and the commitment that excellence demands. The same is true, of course, in the recruitment of coaches. There must be a winner's heart and a willingness to present an unequivocal example. Gable found those qualities, and many more, in Mark Johnson.

Johnson graduated from the University of Michigan, a Big Ten foe of Iowa's, in 1979 and decided to join the Hawkeye Wrestling Club, a club that offers post-graduates an opportunity to prepare and train for world competition. Like scores of wrestlers before him, Mark dreamed of attaining the ultimate award in competitive amateur wrestling, the Olympic gold medal.

"I wanted very badly to make the 1980 Olympic team, and I figured my chances were much greater at Iowa than anyplace else," said Johnson. Time would prove him correct, as Johnson earned a spot on the Greco-Roman Olympic team in the 198-pound weight class.

During his first two years at Iowa, Mark set himself apart from his fellow graduate assistants, not out of vanity but out of maturity. He didn't ride the "bandwagon" to the bars or talk idly about other people. He was a clean-cut, All-American type of guy right from the start, a carry-over from his boyhood and days at Michigan. As the weeks and months ticked away, he soon gained valuable "inside" knowledge and also experienced the Hawkeye recipe for success, a recipe he learned by putting himself through long, torturous and combative workouts, and by meeting the demanding pace set by Gable.

"Coming to Iowa as a college graduate felt like being a freshman again," Johnson recalled in 1984. "Iowa was leagues above everyone else. I felt like I had just graduated from high school, with no college experience, and walked straight into the Iowa mat room."

Yet that was certainly not the case at all. At Michigan Mark had twice been NCAA runnerup at 177 pounds behind Iowa's Chris Campbell (a wrestler Mark defeated in the 1973 junior national tournament in Iowa City). In time Johnson would venture twelve times to distant lands, acquiring the wide degree of experience he was seeking. Yet when first coming to Iowa, Mark found the practices very difficult and demanding.

"I consider it an honor and a compliment for Dan to hire me," said assistant coach Mark Johnson when reflecting back on his first season at Iowa. (Photo by Chuck Yesalis).

"At Michigan our regular practice in season, at full intensity, couldn't compare to Iowa's preseason program," said Johnson. "To me, it's not at all surprising when Iowa finishes number one. They set their goals high and work so damn hard. I'm glad to be a part of this program," he said, a trace of pride evident in his words.

In the same breath, however, he points out that the Iowa program is not meant for all those who come knocking at the door. For many, the price to be paid is simply too steep.

"If you are willing to be here at seven in the morning and leave at seven at night, if you're willing to commit yourself totally starting in October, seven days a week, ending in March at the nationals, then you will probably be a good assistant," said Johnson. "Anything short of those requirements just won't do. Not at Iowa."

Although the commitment is a crucial part of the coaching requirements, there is also a need to add flavor and variety to the program. That is another area Mark excels in.

"Mark is so approachable, so easy to get to know and talk to," said Tim Riley, Iowa's 118- and 126-pounder through 1984. "He knows what we are going through as an athlete because he is still training, too [for the 1984 Olympic Greco-Roman team]. Also, he is very sincere and professional."

I've often felt Mark bridged the gap between the coaches and the athletes; he's the linchpin for a good many of the athletes, and received so much respect from them, and also from Gable. Signs of Dan's confidence in Mark as an official representative of the Iowa wrestling program are clear. With his boyish good looks and friendly smile, Mark is the ideal choice to speak at many banquets—functions essential to the very support of the program.

And then there is the real strength of Mark's involvement. Augmented with his banquet duties are his weight training responsibilities. Gable is very good at utilizing his coaches' strengths,and Mark is a classic example.

Johnson began training with weights on a semi-regular basis in high school in Rock Island, Illinois, and developed a real affinity for the sport in college. As the years passed, thick layers of muscle soon developed on his athletic physique. In addition, he developed a great deal of expertise in the field. Gable soon recognized Mark's wealth of information and gave him free rein in the strength department.

"I'm sure part of the reason Dan hired me is because of my knowledge and love of weights," said Mark candidly. "I like watching guys grow and take pride in their bodies."

Of course, Johnson is able to do far more than provide weight training instruction to the team. Knowing "the system and how Dan wants practice run," he is in charge of practice whenever Gable or Robinson can't make it for pressing reasons, and when the team is on

Mark Johnson developed into one of the nation's most respected amateur wrestlers in his post-graduate days, winning several national titles in both freestyle and Greco-Roman wrestling. He was a member of the 1980 Olympic team in Greco-Roman, at 198 pounds.

the road travelling he is the caretaker of cash that sometimes totals over $4,000, necessary expense money for hotels, food and miscellaneous items. The final compliment to Mark's abilities came early in 1984 when Gable extended his contract for another year and offered him a substantial raise in salary.

"When I was first hired in 1982 I was told the job was for two years," reflected Johnson. "I was ready to pack my belongings and move my wife, Linda, and daughter, Tricia, if Dan thought I was not doing the job. I never really knew where I stood with him until a few days ago. It's a good feeling to know he appreciates my assistance."

Being an assistant coach for such a highly-visible head coach as Dan Gable wouldn't be easy for a good many coaches, but Johnson has never had a problem with working for a man considered a legend. With his calm and collected reasoning, he has had little trouble assessing the program and his role in it.

"I didn't have to be Iowa's assistant," he said matter of factly. "I had a fine job in Sarasota, Florida, as the director of a boys' club in a YMCA. Plus, I was really enjoying the chance to compete in bodybuilding [Johnson has won two physique contests and placed high in several other major ones] and the Florida weather was not hard to take. In the final analysis, it wasn't the money that was important; it was the opportunity to be around winners and hard workers that appealed to me. Plus, being around and learning from Gable. He is infectious; he is a doer. Gable brought wrestling out of the Dark Ages and into the media's eye, and the public's eye. It was a big step and was made possible mostly by Gable himself."

Not only has Gable brought wrestling out of the Dark Ages and into the spotlight, but he has also brought new meaning to the word "coach." He is not stagnant as a coach, but is constantly striving to become better each dual meet, each tournament, each season.

"I don't feel 'special' if I'm putting guys through technique or weight training sessions at seven in the morning when Dan is there at five a.m. putting Ed Banach, Tim Riley and Harlan Kistler through workouts," said Mark, who adds that Gable is unique in his ability to deal with each wrestler's personality and motivational needs.

"Dan has really gone through an evolution. He started by training himself, and now he has learned to deal with individuals who are very different from himself. He has learned to treat Rico different than Pete Bush, and Lou Banach different than Ed Banach. It is one very important example of his growth, and greatness, as a coach, and an example I try to use in my own coaching as much as possible.

"Before this year [the 1983-84 season], Rico wouldn't touch weights," said Johnson, who has been described as the strongest wrestler in the world. "Probably he would have fared better in the Big Ten and NCAA meets his freshman year if he would have. Anyway,

Bodybuilding and strength training are two more areas in which Mark Johnson excels. He has been featured in national magazines and has placed first or second in some of the top bodybuilding meets in the Midwest and Florida.

last year I don't think Rico could bench press 135 pounds, strength that is necessary for pummelling and pushing.

"But this year I found the secret to getting Rico into weight training. Rico likes to look at himself in mirrors, so I had mirrors put up in the weight room, and also gave him some bodybuilding magazines. I can just see him picturing mentally that he can be as big as Frank Zane or Arnold Schwarzenegger," laughed Johnson. "Most guys could care less about the mirrors, but Rico's case is different. They keep attracting him to the weight room. He's done so well in his weight training that he can now bench press 275 pounds. That's tremendous progress."

That example brings home once again the unique aspect of the Iowa wrestling program: The coaches, as well as the wrestlers, recognize the challenges before them and are constantly striving to improve, on all levels.

Another example of the dedication of the coaching staff came in Bethlehem, Pennsylvania, following a one-point escape of the Hawks from a fired-up Lehigh team. Gable summoned all coaches and wrestlers to the locker room for a postmatch talk. He was white with anger, for he firmly believes no team should come within ten points of Iowa. He felt the Engineers had just outmuscled and outmanned the Hawks.

Understanding the handwriting on the wall, a concerned Johnson was quick to assess the situation and offer a solution.

"Hey, I'll be glad to meet any of you guys at six a.m., eight a.m., or ten p.m., whatever it takes," said Mark firmly. "Just tell me when and I'll be there to put you through the weights. I'll make the effort if you will. All you have to do is say when and where."

His complete willingness to give of his time and knowledge and his long-term commitment to excellence are two of the many reasons Gable so firmly believes in Mark, as an athlete as well as a coach. Through wrestling, Mark has grown into manhood. He has learned the importance of setting goals, overcoming defeat and disciplining himself. Both weight training/bodybuilding and wrestling have taught him the necessity for diet control and abstinence, and the benefits of a disciplined way of life. He understands the many values of wrestling: "It's a sport that teaches you to survive in life," he said, "and at Iowa, wretlers prove constantly that through hard work, discipline and dedication you can be successful. Iowa wrestling is an armor against life and defeat."

Johnson also admits he has learned one of life's most valuable lessons from Gable.

"People ask me his secret all the time," said Mark. "It's so simple, really. Dan outworked everyone as a wrestler, and he outworks everyone as a coach. The truth is there for everyone to see, if they will just open up their eyes and see it. Hard work. That's what makes Iowa."

It's a theme that is preached over and over and over in this book, because it is the thread that holds the Iowa program together: it's the work ethic that Gable, Robinson and Johnson subscribe to, and that all the wrestlers must come to grips with.

At Iowa one learns to adapt and grow, if he will allow himself to. Paul Wiederman, a graduate of Harvard, passed up medical school to come to Iowa to train for the Olympics. He wanted to train with Gable and the Hawks.

"Iowa is a place where one can go and almost be assured of success if he puts in the commitment and has the desire," he said. That desire and commitment are exemplified most honorably in the person of Mark Johnson, Olympic athlete and Hawkeye coach, really one of the new breed.

Dan Gable:

Searching for the Man

The wrestling office at the University of Iowa is situated in the bowels of the Carver-Hawkeye Sports Arena, a brand new and attractive labyrinth named for millionaire philanthropist Roy Carver and for the symbol of Iowa athletics, a Hawkeye. To reach the wrestling office, you descend two levels beneath street level and walk along a carpeted corridor lined with photos of national champions. They are not little four-by-five photos, but large, twelve-by-fifteen color prints, and there are twelve of them in all, dating back to the first of the new breed, Dan Shorman (the ex-Illinois prep who won the 118-pound title in 1972).

Wrestling is special here at Iowa, and is treated accordingly. After the corridor, you enter the main portion of the wrestling office, a good-sized room with a number of partitions providing a certain amount of privacy for the various coaches and secretaries. Still, it is easy to see others when they arrive, and conversations are easily overheard.

On this occasion, I am looking for Dan Gable, and I find him on the telephone. He is playing nervously with his fingers. Remembering our conversation of a few days earlier, he motions for me to take a seat.

His pace increases: He answers several calls, plays with pencils, twists his fingers, and chats with various world team members (the tryouts for the World Freestyle Championships have just been held in the Iowa wrestling room, and the team is training here before departing for Kiev, Soviet Union) as they shuffle by. For a moment I think I understand what it must be like to be Dan Gable. He is a man with many, many demands on him; he is saddled with wrestling commitments, business commitments, personal commitments and, of course, family commitments. He seems to be always on the move, always preoccupied. I wonder—does he ever have an idle moment, time to spend just being a person?

The same intensity that made Dan Gable America's most-talked about collegiate wrestler ever has made him the most successful coach ever. Above, with fists clenched, Gable displays his enthusiasm during a dual meet at Iowa. (Photo by Greg Mellis).

Sitting there observing my coach, I find myself contemplating his motivations, particularly in wrestling. Questions arise: What is the source of his behavior, what directs or channels it? How can this behavior, born of intense determination and drive and apparently immune to pain and fatigue, be sustained? To find the answers is, of course, part of the mission I am on, one of the purposes of this book; without his knowledge, the book would be a skeleton without flesh without blood.

Gable sits calmly at his oversized desk in his somewhat oversized chair. It's easy to forget how small he really is, because he always seems much larger than his 5-9, 160-pound frame. On the practice floor visitors always look for a man who weighs 200 pounds and is six feet tall. I am struck by the fact his desk and chair seem out of place in a wrestling office; they seem more appropriate to the office of a president of a highly successful business. But then I realize once again that is exactly the type of office I am sitting in, and the type of office Gable is running; Iowa wrestling is big business, and Gable is the president of the corporation, the chairman of the board, the man in charge—total charge.

Gable's voice cuts through my reflections:

"We may have to take a train for twenty-four straight hours," he says to the listener on the other end of the phone hookup. The trip to the Soviet Union is coming just weeks after the Soviets shot down a Korean jetliner with 297 people aboard. They all died, and an international incident of tremendous scope is brewing. The wrestlers are finding themselves right in the middle of it. Flights in and out of the Soviet Union have been severely restricted, and the trip is in jeopardy. At the very least, it will be a rough and mentally draining sojourn for the American matmen. But Gable shows why he may have the most fantastic outlook of any coach in the world. He takes a negative situation and makes it positive. The long train trip, dreaded by everyone, is put into a new perspective by Gable.

That'll be good for their mental toughness," he says to his listener, referring to his world team's state of mind. Suddenly you find yourself believing it, too. Perhaps that is Gable's greatest magic.

It's a good place for me to delve into his subconscious, I reason. I ask him why he is so energetic, why he always seems so motivated. It's a process which never seems to stop, and has no ending.

"A man has got to do something with his life," he says in that straightforward manner you come to associate with Gable. He is a man who seems totally incapable of bending the truth. He hates falsehoods every bit as much as he hates losing. If you ever want to incur the wrath of Dan Gable, lie to him, and have him find you out.

"Mine is wrestling," he says, of his life's mission. "I'm no different from a businessman who wants a million dollars. I just want wrestling champions."

There it is—plain truth. But is it really that simple? I offer that surely countless other coaches must have that very same goal, yet fall short.

"Yeah, but they aren't serious about it," comes his retort. "You've got to feel we are here on earth for a reason. I tried a lot of other sports—swimming, baseball—but they weren't my niche. Wrestling was a sport that I could excel at. My parents had a big role. They showed me, gave me the chance to grow.

"They kicked me in the butt when I needed it, made sure I did my homework, made sure I learned good, honorable habits. I guess as each year passed my habits became more hardened. Today, if I don't work out or keep busy at the office, I go crazy. I need work, need wrestling."

I felt an opening for an obvious question. Gable, after leading his team to six straight NCAA team titles and a dual meet record of 122-5-2, was being criticized in some circles. His successes, it was said, were at the expense of wrestling. He was destroying the very sport he loved by building an empire that no other school could compete with. He was allegedly ruining the sport.

"Well, some coaches don't think so, but I do," he responds, his face set in an expression of cocky pride. "Every sport needs an example, like Ali in boxing. I am the example for wrestling, right now."

Do you want to be the example, I asked.

"At times I don't," he says, "but I believe that's God's purpose for me. If I can pass on words of clean living, developing habits for youngsters, then I feel I'm doing my bit." He lowers his voice, so that others might not hear, and continues: "Just look around, look at our bodies, look at our position in life. There is no way anyone can convince me that there isn't a God. We're just too complex."

Then his voice changes, and rises. He is on a roll now: "Hey, you got to believe—that's what pulls me through the matches, the interviews and life. I have faith in what I'm doing. If you can work hard, never complain, do your part, then you can be happy. I don't cheat anyone; I don't complain. I just go about my life in my fashion."

It's now suddenly very clear why Gable, Robinson and Johnson work so well together as a staff. They have a common credo for life, and it's their work ethic. All are from the same mold, the exact same mold. Robinson believes in working harder than the next fellow. So does Johnson. If you ask Johnson what makes Gable so successful, he says everyone else as a coach," says Johnson. "It's that simple."

Simple, in definition, yet incredibly hard in performance. To outwork Dan Gable may in fact be impossible.

"If I was another wrestling coach anywhere in this country, I would really be depressed," says Russ Camilleri, a thirteen-time national champion who returned to wrestling at the age of 46 in the fall of 1983, and chose the Iowa workout room to try to recapture his once considerable skills. "I have been in programs all over the country for years, but I've never seen anything like Dan Gable. He is a genius, the absolute best—ever. No one else is even in his league. He just plain outworks everyone and it carries over to his kids, anyone who's around him. It's a new era."

"I have done no wrong with wrestling," says Gable. I had my goals, and I worked at them. I got what I deserve. I think others are getting what they deserve, too. Mediocrity breeds mediocrity. I'm breeding winners in wrestling, and life. I think that's what The Man Upstairs wants from me. To make my kids tough and ready for life."

Suddenly, the interview is over, Gable jumps up. "Is that it?" he asks. Yes, for now, I respond. Thanks!

His mind is now on his team, his world team. He yells out to them that it's time for the pictures to be taken for the passports.

The abruptness of Gable's actions reminds me of a recent story written about him. He said he doesn't want anyone getting too close to him, to know him too well. When that happens, he said, he retreats. I have just seen him retreat. Perhaps he knows he has given too much of himself away. . . .

What Gable is to a nation of wrestling followers is a leader of unshaken dimensions. Not all have accepted his leadership, but those who have have benefitted remarkably well.

General Creighton W. Abrams, chief of staff from 1972 to 1974, U.S. Army, expressed it this way: "There must be, within ourself, a sense of purpose. There must be a willingness to march a little further, to carry a heavier load, to step out into the dark and the unknown for the safety and well-being of others."

Gable has stepped out into the dark, and has survived. He has not only survived, but dedicated himself to leading others on the same perilous path to self-knowledge and fulfillment.

In reflection, Gable survives as a legend—a living legend. Maybe for that single reason, it is extremely difficult for him to seem "human," to let his hair down and to show the inner being to the world.

He exists as a man caught between being a legend and being a man. So he must retreat at times, not only to be himself but to renew the relationship between himself and the man he is deep beneath the legend.

As he walks away from me in that shuffle that he has developed, dragging his feet almost like a little boy would, he turns and tells me to "read the magazine on my desk—there's an article on me. It should help."

Actually, the entire magazine—the Sunday supplement for *The Des Moines Register*, called "Picture"—is about Gable. On the cover there is a color photo of Dan holding his baby while the Gables are visiting their cabin on the Mississippi River, some 80 miles northeast of Iowa City. The cabin is where Gable retreats when he wants to escape the microscope under which he spends a good deal of his life. Here he can be just plain old Dan Gable—open, relaxed, humorous and content. Here he finds the balance with being a legend. Realizing people won't—or can't—accept him as a person with feelings, he has found his freedom, his peace, his balance.

When I earlier asked Gable what was in his future, he didn't hesitate: "My family," he says. "My job—my time in the sport—is limited."

For years Gable ruled the wrestling room—any one he walked into. For over a decade he could defeat any man, regardless of weight, skill or intent. National champ or world champ, it made no difference. He was the king. But naturally even those days faded. The day in which he could physically whip any wrestler on the team is gone. Dan knows it and is trying to accept the feeling. Alongside that realization are the creeping problems, such as constant pains from old mat injuries. With all of this to contend with, you'd think he'd be sour.

Though Gable has become a legend in the athletic world, he is a devout family man. He and his wife, Kathy, have three daughters — Jennifer, Annie and Molly. (Photo by Chuck Yesalis).

But you'd be wrong. Even though he once won 180 straight matches in high school and collegiate-style wrestling, even though he won two world championships back-to-back, even though he won six straight Midlands titles and was the outstanding wrestler five times, even though he was called the greatest pinner in collegiate history by *Amateur Wrestling News* in 1970 and is considered now, by most wrestling aficionados, to be the biggest name in the history of the sport. Gable's greatest triumph may be subsumed in his attitude toward . . . not wrestling, but life.

"I'm happy," he says with conviction. "I can walk, run—hell, I'm healthy. Just go over to the University of Iowa Hospitals and see all the cripples. That's sad. Sure, I'm banged up, but that's part of the game. If it isn't a give-and-take situation, it wouldn't be fair or realistic."

Then he catches me off guard.

"Hey, the grass isn't greener on the other side of the fence. Too many people think it is. I'm just content. I've got a livelihood, a healthy family and fine friends. Sure, it's not everything, but I'm satisfied."

On the surface Gable is a complex man. But inside he is very simple. He enjoys his life, his fame and his role in wrestling. He is not asking others to change, just to accept him and his Hawks.

And he offers the ultimate example for wrestlers.

"Dan Gable did more to promote and popularize the sport of amateur wrestling than any single individual in the history of the sport," said ex-Arizona coach Bill Nelson several years ago. "He demonstrated what total dedication, sacrifice and hard work can accomplish."

That is the legacy of Gable—to wrestlers at Iowa, across the nation and around the world. It's a message wrapped with such principles as faith in God, commitment and dedication; but, the message is this, true and simple: Work as hard as humanly possible, and believe in yourself.

It's a message he left with me, and one that I will look to for the remainder of my life.

The Making of a Champion

When wrestling fans gather to discuss their sport, talk invariably gets around to Iowa, and several questions always come up. Why does Iowa always seem to finish number one in the nation, winning six straight NCAA team championships, and eight in the last nine years? How come this team seems to get better and better each succeeding year?

In 1978 the Hawks won at Maryland by one-fourth of a point over Iowa State University. In each of the following years, once the smoke had cleared, no team had come within fifteen points. Then at the 1983 NCAA meet in Oklahoma City, Oklahoma State University finished second with a school record 102 points—yet it was still 53 points behind the incredible 155 points rolled up by the Hawkeyes. In winning the title by the largest margin in NCAA history, Iowa crowned four national champions, had one second-place finish, two thirds and a fourth. It was a spellbinding performance.

The Gazette **Sports**

Cedar Rapids/Saturday, March 12, 1983

Section B

Outdoor	4B
Comics	6B
Money	7B
Stock Listings	8-9B
Farm	10B

Gable's men make it 6 straight!

Sign man

By Mike Chapman
Gazette sports editor

EAST LANSING, Mich. — Maybe your television set didn't show them, but there were several signs in Michigan's Crisler Arena Thursday night that entertained the Michigan fans.

The signs were painted by a Michigan booster. You have to give him credit for originality, even if you don't applaud his messages.

At halftime he held up one that read: "Iowa — best talent, best chokes." When that drew hardy guffaws from Wolverine faithful, the guy showed 'em the flip side. "Lute — best hair, worst coach."

A friend from Ann Arbor noticed us reading the signs and said, "Maybe Iowa's coach is getting off easy. When Coach Bobby Knight brought his Indiana team here, the guy had a dandy sign that said, 'Big Ten refs — incompetent by day, intimidated by Knight.' That brought some great howls of delight."

You would expect people traveling with the Iowa team to be sympathetic to the Hawkeyes and their coaches, and they were after Michigan stormed back in the

OKLAHOMA CITY, Okla — Once again, for the sixth straight year the Iowa Hawkeyes rule the world of college wrestling.

Oh sure, there's more wrestling to be done today as the 53rd NCAA championships draw to a close. But that's to determine the individual place winners

Radio station KCJJ (1560 AM) of Iowa City will broadcast live tonight (beginning at 6:55) the championship matches involving Iowa wrestlers.

The Hawkeyes of Coach Dan Gable took care of the teams race late Friday night. Wrestling in the Myriad Convention Center in the semifinal round, the Hawks put on another of their powerful displays.

Nine of the 10 Iowa matmen will place in the top eight. Five of them — Barry Davis, 126; Jim Zalesky, 158; Duane Goldman, 177; Ed Banach, 190, and Lou Banach, heavyweight — will go for championships.

In addition, Tim Riley, 118; Jeff Kerber, 134; Harlan Kistler, 142, and Jim Heffernan,

150, are in today's consolation matches and will earn place winnings.

The team scoring after Friday's semifinal matches had Iowa with 121.75 points, followed by Iowa State with 81.75 and Oklahoma State with 80.25. Oklahoma was a far distant fourth with 52.75 points.

The Cyclones of Iowa State have three finalists, and two of them face Hawks. At 190,

Lou Banach gets sweet revenge against Oklahoma State heavyweight Mitch Shelton. Page 2B.

Mike Mann tries for his fourth straight win over Ed Banach, while at heavyweight, Wayne Cole will try for his first win over Lou Banach in six meetings.

"I wrestled real good against (Nebraska's Bill) Scherr, and I'll go home and sleep on it tonight," said Ed Banach. "I'll go out tomorrow and wrestle my butt off because I want to win. Mann has beaten me three times and I want it to change. I'm gonna take it to him."

An Iowa State assistant coach said Mann was very tense and would appreciate no reporters' questions until after the finals.

Should Ed win the match, he would become the first three-time NCAA champion in Iowa history.

At 150, Nate Carr will try to become the second three-time NCAA champion for Iowa State when he takes on Oklahoma State's Ken Monday. The pair have split in two previous meetings this season.

Cyclones still able to score team points in the consolation finals this afternoon are John Thorn at 118, Kevin Darkus at 126, Randy Conrad at 142 and Murray Crews at 158.

Thorn turned in the biggest upset of the tournament on Friday's quarterfinal action when he edged top-seeded and previously unbeaten Randy Willingham of Oklahoma State, 8-7. Just two weeks ago, Willingham had beaten Thorn at the Big Eight meet 24-7.

Then, Iowa's Riley nipped Willingham in the consolation wrestlebacks, 3-3, 1-1 criteria decision, to knock the Cowboy star completely out of the field.

Zalesky

Davis

Iowa entered the semifinal round with an unbelievable 29.2 record. It put eight men in the semis, but lost three. At 134, Kerber bowed to Oklahoma's Clinton Burke, 7-3, and at 142 Harlan Kistler was defeated by Nebraska star Al Freeman, 11-3. Then

• *Please turn to page 3B.* Gable

NCAA or NIT?
Hawkeyes finish
at MSU tonight

By Gus Schrader
Gazette sports columnist

So what is the recipe, the secret behind Iowa's staggering successes? Is it Gable, or the combination of Gable-Robinson-Johnson? Is it the great fan support? In reality it is all of the above, and more.

The state of Iowa has no professional sports teams, and therefore, the fans have a strong allegiance and loyalty to University of Iowa athletic teams. The fans provide the financial backing and moral support so vital to good athletic teams. The football team suffered through twenty straight non-winning seasons until the arrival of Hayden Fry in 1979. Yet during that time Kinnick Stadium was nearly always filled to capacity as over 60,000 loyal fans trudged to the stadium each fall to support a team that was far less than adequate. For the past three years, with Fry taking Iowa to three straight bowl appearances, Hawkeye fever has run rampant. Iowa is thought to be the only school in America where both the football season tickets and the basketball season tickets sell out completely before the start of each season.

And Iowa fans love their wrestling. They have always had an appreciation for this most rugged of collegiate sports, yet it wasn't until Gary Kurdelmeier took over the head job in 1973 that the interest in Iowa wrestling really blossomed. Years ago, Iowa used to wrestle in a secondary gym off to the side of the main arena to crowds of less than two hundred people. But Kurdelmeier changed all of that, promoting wrestling as one would a winning football team, and elevating his sport, through the news media, into a highly visible position. When he named Dan Gable as his assistant, Iowa fans sat up and took notice. When the Hawks won their first-ever NCAA wrestling team championship in 1975, the program had a whole flock of new wrestling fans, many who had climbed aboard the bandwagon partly because they were so hungry for a winner.

Eventually the old Fieldhouse saw capacity crowds for the Iowa State meets, with over 12,000 rabid fans cheering wildly for their team. In addition, traditional powers like Oklahoma State, Oklahoma, and even Wisconsin and Lehigh would occasionally draw crowds of close to 10,000. It was great timing—success and the desire to support a winner came together in a perfect blend. The victory-starved Iowa fans wanted a winner, and Kurdelmeier and Gable delivered.

Gable has a formula, one that is really quite simple. He feels to be successful as a team, the coach, stressing that wrestling is an individual sport, must work on each wrestler individually to become the best wrestler possible. Gable and Kurdelmeier established the Hawkeye Wrestling Club, which was designed to offer post-graduates an opportunity to train, and undergraduates the opportunity to gain from the invaluable experiences of the older

Dan Gable as a wrestler: At Iowa State, Gable stretched his unbeaten streak (counting high school and college-style matches) to 180 in a row. His junior year as a Cyclone, he pinned 26 of 28 foes, defeating the other two by scores of 25-6 and 12-1.

matmen. In time these veterans would make an incredible difference in the Iowa team, as it was like having an extra twelve coaches in the room. The experience and knowledge of the veterans was passed on to the younger Hawks. The development of the club was one of the biggest keys in the Hawkeye success story.

Perhaps the club's biggest impact was the manner in which it allowed people to become involved with wrestling. There were many jobs to be done, and Kurdelmeier and Gable were effective in delegating assignments and getting people involved in wrestling. It made them feel like they had something to contribute to and something to belong to. In 1984 Gable told a radio audience that the club was one of the most important elements to Iowa's success over the years.

The Hawkeye Wrestling Club received an undeniable boost in its infancy from multi-millionaire Roy Carver, but his role in the Iowa wrestling program, at all levels, has been vastly overestimated by those outside the program. The strength of the club has always been in the large number of "average" fans who wanted to become involved through volunteer work and small contributions. When Carver died in 1981, his loss was felt, but the club still prospered and developed.

"I had an interesting experience when I worked at Veteran's Hospital [in Iowa City] years ago," related Kurdelmeier. "I observed the volunteer program there, and it amazed me how people would work for love and not for pay. It became obvious to me that there are people who have a great love for the sport. When I came, I tried to gather a group of people who wanted to work for love, not money. We gave them a chance to become involved with a top wrestling program."

That was the "secret" ingredient of the Iowa Wrestling Club. It is one that the enterprising coach, at any level, can put to work for him and his program—if he's willing to work at it as Kurdelmeier did.

Iowa, of course, is not the only college to build a club contact. The University of Oklahoma has its Underdog Club, Iowa State its Cyclone Club, Arizona State the Sunkist Kids, Cal Bakersfield the Bakersfield Express, and Lehigh is affiliated with the New York Athletic Club. Wisconsin, Northern Iowa and Northwestern are other schools trying to build clubs.

At Iowa the Club has branched out to other activities. It has been involved with clinics, hosting tournaments, supporting charitable organizations (such as the multiple sclerosis and epilepsy foundations), and it sponsors get-togethers after most of Iowa's home dual meets. It's not uncommon to attend a post-meet party that has attracted over several hundred wrestling backers.

After the formation of the club, Gable began the search for a new breed of athlete. He wasn't concerned if a recruit was not physically strong, lacked technique or was short on conditioning. All Gable was really searching for was the right attitude. He wanted an attitude born of a certain mental toughness, an attitude that would allow the athlete to prevail in a damanding practice or in a match. He wanted a wrestler with heart, one who was willing to go that extra mile to be a champ.

The old adage that one bad apple can spoil the entire basket is true, but Gable reversed it: He felt one good apple could make a dramatic difference in the entire team. Dan himself was the best of these good apples, bringing with him into the program his insatiable thirst for excellence and incredible training discipline, and soon guys like Brad Smith, Dan Holm, Bruce Kinseth and John Bowlsby showed up. They had the determination and the will not only to win, but to pay the price that was necessary.

The wheel was turning once these athletes arrived. Like most changes, it would take time. But these hungry, aggressive wrestlers kept pouring in. Behind Smith, Holm, Bowlsby and Brad Smith came Mike DeAnna, Scott Trizzino, Dan Glenn and Randy Lewis, all wanting to be the very best, and all willing to pay just about any price. Suddenly Gable had a basketfull of good apples. They all were eager to run and lift and drill, not just wrestle. They had acquired the most difficult trait of all, a good work ethic. Work became a habit to them. Though they enjoyed their off-mat time, they still established priorities, and the workouts came first, far and away. In 1978, Gable's second year as head coach, the Hawks gave him his first NCAA team title, after winning two with Kurdelmeier as head coach.

Gable's hard work and building continued. His education as a coach continued, as well, and he continued to develop on the job. The simple recipe was paying off in staggering dividends now, with contagious hard work and enthusiasm the key ingredients.

The Iowa program seldom recruits junior college athletes because the coaches believe it is important for a wrestler to have the benefit of four or five years in the Iowa system. It is very difficult for an athlete with two years of college experience behind him to step into the Iowa program and make the adjustment to the high levels of work and commitment.

The commitment to excellence is not something confined to the "varsity" lineup at Iowa. When Iowa gets into the tough part of the season, with two- and three-a-day workouts, not just the starting ten are expected at each morning practice, but the other members of the team, as well. Many foes have a high regard (bordering on fear, in some instances) for Iowa's conditioning, both mental and physical, and that conditioning was earned through extra long and grueling workouts. Part of the reason the Hawks are in such good shape is that their workout partners push them to new limits.

Gable sets his limits, too. He knows a wrestler will tire eventually; that's only normal. But it's the wrestler who can put the fatigue out of his mind and break through the "wall," like a marathon runner after eighteen or twenty miles, who will survive. The key to that survival is in hard workouts that develop mental confidence to the point where you won't submit to the fatigue and pain descending upon you.

The great football coach Vince Lombardi once said that "fatigue makes cowards of us all." That's certainly true. But we can learn to control the fatigue factor; without a doubt, fatigue can be mastered and overcome by conditioning. It's a big price to pay—but it's worth it!

Gable schemes up practices that will drain every wrestler completely and build confidence in conditioning; these very special days are known as red-flag days.

The red-flag day epitomizes Gable's love of hard work, and inspires fear in even the most hardened wrestlers. It involves 70-80 straight minutes of wrestling, running and sprints, with no letup. Constant motion. I have never been through anything more demanding in my life. Once, Mike DeAnna came into the locker room, stripped and walked to the scales to check his weight. There, posted

In his job as the Iowa wrestling coach, Dan Gable continued to grow and to mature, understanding that not all athletes could meet his own commitment to the sport. The new breed of athletes were helping to develop a new breed of coach. (Photo courtesy of the *Cedar Rapids Gazette*).

on the front of the scale, was the notice that it was red-flag day. Without hesitating, Mike redressed and scampered out of the locker room. He's certainly not the only wrestler to ever have avoided a red-flag day.

But red-flag days are something special, although I usually lost nearly ten pounds, and the lighter-weight guys lose between six and eight pounds.

What was satisfying about the workout is that after Gable's hand — the symbolic red flag — went up, signalling a breather, everyone let out a sigh of relief—and contentment. I know that as a team we grew closer after each workout; red-flag days really pull a team together. Even the coaches participate; it is a total team effort. Sure, we're exhausted physically, but mentally we know we went through and survived hell. With the temperature in the room near 105 degrees and the humidity around 90 percent, we pushed our battered and sweaty partners to the very limit—a limit few people will ever reach, or know.

And that is uniquely Iowa. To establish the pace, to set a new standard in commitment and intensity. During these workouts one gets a sort of "high." It doesn't feel good physically, but mentally it leaves you content. That is if you're not wrestling Gable.

Red-flag days are, of course, merely symbolic, as there are no red flags in evidence in the Iowa wrestling room. But the impact of red-flag days is real enough. My brother Steve, a fine and rugged athlete in his own right, went to Ranger school after leaving Iowa, and readily admitted red-flag days helped him tremendously.

"What we went through in Ranger school was tough," said Steve, "but not as tough as red-flag days at Iowa. I felt I was prepared for anything after making it through those workouts back in Iowa City."

Red-flag days are the extreme, but wrestling for Iowa on a day-to-day basis is very difficult. The intensity in the workouts carries over into the tryout matches. It has been said some of the best wrestling matches in the nation take place in the Iowa wrestling room, and I believe it. Often the loser could go to another school and break the lineup with ease, and probably place in the national tournament. We have had national place-winners and Big Ten champions fail to make the team the following season.

Steve Banach transferred to Iowa from Clemson University, where he was Atlantic Coast Conference runner-up as a sophomore. Yet he could never quite crack the Iowa lineup, losing close matches to Pete Bush, who became NCAA champion. King Mueller, third in the nation at 150 pounds as a junior, and Dean Phinney, third in the NCAA tourney at heavyweight, were not able to regain starting spots their senior years. Several junior college national champions have come to Iowa, only to sit on the bench and never wrestle for the varsity.

When a wrestler makes the team, Gable gives him one or two months to wrestle. If the progress is good and the wrestler is winning and improving, then Gable usually won't grant any additional tryouts to the challengers. It's a method that seems to work well for Iowa. But every two or three weeks each wrestler is tested in various ways in matches. By testing through competition and tournaments, wrestlers become immune to the pressure. This is not true for all: Mark Mysnyk and Steve Banach had difficulty in the high-pressure wrestling arena, but both have gone on to be successful in life. To Gable, practice sessions are not an effective way to evaluate an athlete, because the wrestler tends to place too much emphasis on making the team and neglects preparing for the opponent.

Gable is of course concerned with conditioning, but even more important, he feels, is the building of confidence in the wrestler and the establishment of team unity. He feels that allowing a new wrestler to take a spot in the lineup every other week or so, will lessen both unity and the individual wrestler's confidence.

Our team is usually set by February, which is important because each wrestler needs to have his weaknesses assessed and worked on. Having the lineup set by February allows four or so weeks of intense work before tournament time rolls around. Gable wants his athletes to improve, and he knows improvement only comes about through hard work. The entire season is geared around the national

Even Hawkeyes are allowed to rest once in a while. But when they do, they stick together, showing their team unity. Above, several of them relax between sessions of the 1983 Big Ten Championships in Iowa City. (Photo courtesy of the *Cedar Rapids Gazette*).

tournament, on titles for the team and individual titles, because they are what is important. Folks may forget what happened in the various dual meets or in the conference tournament, but win the nationals and they will remember you. Sam Komar at Indiana is an excellent example. He was 14-14 in dual meets, but was NCAA runnerup at 142 pounds in 1977.

To be number one demands not only discipline but also the will power to form good work habits and maintain them, to work out when friends are going to the movie, or when everyone else is sleeping. To set the ball rolling at Iowa, we had Gable to emulate. He was the prime example, and we all learned from him. One old-time coach was quoted once as saying Gable showed the way for all wrestlers to follow, that he was proof that incredible hard work and dedication could take anyone to the top. He learned he can teach us all the technique and mat strategy and offer the inspiration, but it is still up to each individual to make the commitment to hard work. If anyone doesn't, then he knows he will be just another athlete.

But again, the key element to success is work. On and off the mat, Iowa sets the standard. Few men have come to realize that fact better than Mark Mysnyk, a three-time New York state champion who came to Iowa as a heralded prep star, and now is a doctor in residence at University of Iowa Hospitals. He captured the essence of Gable, and the dream of all Hawkeye matmen, with the following words:

"Most men stop when they begin to tire. Good men go until they think they are going to collapse. But the very best know the mind tires before the body, and push themselves further and further, beyond all limits. Only when these limits are shattered can the unattainable be reached."

That philosophy is the heart of the Iowa wrestling program.

The Hawkeye recipe is simple: Work hard each day, put in quality time, talk to the coaches and tap their great reservoirs of experience, set your goals high and work toward them with total dedication. And if you pace yourself throughout the long season as though you were in a marathon, you'll finish strong—a finish that could have you standing at the top of the awards platform at the NCAA tournament or at the Olympics. It is a recipe that knows no shortcuts to success. The way to the top is through your commitment to self, team and sport!

The advice and technique included in this chapter can certainly help make anyone an excellent wrestler. Being the best, though, requires mental toughness.

The following formula for success was devised by Gable when he was in training, and has evolved through the years. It made him a champion of unparalleled dimensions, and can help you to scale the heights, if you are willing to accept its rules, and to persevere. Here it is, in step-by-step form.

1. There is no substitute for hard work. That is the basic fact of life that flows through all of Gable's philosophy. Accept that, and you have won half the battle.

2. Use failure to better yourself. Everyone will fail at one time or another. That is the nature of athletics, and it is inevitable. But what you do *after* you fail is the measure of a champion. Through the years, Gable seldom experienced losing himself (he once won 180 straight matches in high school and college wrestling, and his overall career record was 305-7), but he understood it well enough to help athletes like Davis, Fitzgerald and the Banachs bounce back from defeat.

3. Try your hardest when in a match. It is not critical if you win all the early dual matches or tournaments, but it *is* important you continue to improve over the season so you are ready both mentally and physically for the NCAA tournament, the final testing ground.

4. Conceive, believe, achieve. This is Dan's mental strategy. Just as lifting weights makes the muscles stronger, so do conceiving and believing make the mind stronger. Gable wants an athlete to conceive of a goal, then believe he can attain it through hard work, discipline and commitment. If you can exercise this thought 100 times in your mind, repeating it over and over just as you would an exercise, then you'll be better prepared to obtain your goal. The Iowa coaches believe this so fervently that each season they bring a psychologist from Chicago to work on it with the athletes, stressing mental imagery and positive thinking.

5. Study your opponent, at each tourney and by videotapes. Gene Tunney used this technique to perfection when preparing for his epic clash with Jack Dempsey, who was one of the most feared fighters to ever step in a ring. Tunney plotted Dempsey's every move for two years, then went into the ring and boxed him senseless, lifting the title in a classic upset. Gable reasons one shouldn't go into a college classroom test unprepared, nor should one enter a match that way.

6. Accept injuries and learn to work around them—in fact, injuries may help you to become a better wrestler. If you have a bad ankle, then forget training on your feet for a period and work on the mat. The end result is that your mat wrestling will undoubtedly improve.

7. Set your goals *high*. Don't be satisfied with a dual meet victory, even if it's in a meet like Iowa-Iowa State. Strive for the top. Don't sell yourself short. Shoot for the NCAA title, and if you don't achieve that, you still will have benefitted from setting a lofty goal and working hard for it. That is a quality that can carry over into other areas of your life.

8. Learn patience, and utilize it. The martial arts teach that patience can be a great virtue. A marathon runner knows that he can't start off the 26 miles in a dead sprint. There is a certain amount of pacing that must be put into effect for a long wrestling season, and patience is the key.

9. Coaches must treat each athlete as an individual, trying to understand how and why he is motivated. Not all athletes compete for the same reasons, and the coach who understands that, and attempts to understand his athletes' motivation, will get the most out of them. They can polish what they do well, and trim what they do not do well. Athletics should educate the coach as well as the athlete.

10. Coaches must market their programs. They are in business—a highly competitive business to attract fans and find financial backing. They need to stimulate an interest in their program through whatever means are available—speeches, kids' clinics, summer tournaments, posters with the season's schedules, fan clubs.

Those are the basics of Iowa's wrestling success. Hard work, a desire for understanding, and proper goal setting can take you and your program to the pinnacle of success, too.

Gable is rough on himself in setting goals—such as his professed desire to crown ten Big Ten champs (he had nine in 1983) and ten NCAA champs (he had four in 1983)—because he believes it makes him a better person and a better coach. Making the goals so high they are difficult to obtain strengthens the resolve of the wrestler.

Gable has always set his goals as high as his imagination would allow. After he won his first state title as a skinny 95-pounder at West

High School in Waterloo, Iowa, he began dreaming of the NCAA title. After winning his NCAA title, his mind turned to the world—and he became the first American to ever win back-to-back world championships. As a wrestler, Gable's goal was to always run one mile farther than anyone else, to wrestle ten minutes longer in the room, to pay the price he knew others would not pay. His goal was to succeed, no matter the price. He was never content as a wrestler, and is seldom content as a coach. Even as his Hawks captured their sixth straight NCAA team title in 1983, his mind was on the Soviets, and his goal was to bring home the team championship for the Americans in the 1984 Olympic Games in Los Angeles.

The irony about Gable's accomplishments is that other wrestling coaches have attacked him, absurdly claiming that he hurts the sport he has devoted his life to, because his teams so thoroughly dominate it. Because his "business" is prospering, they feel theirs is suffering. Instead of trying to learn from and emulate his success, they downgrade it, hoping to gain sympathy for their inadequacies. His detractors claim he has so much money and support at his disposal at Iowa that it is difficult for him *not* to win. Yet what they conveniently overlook is the long, arduous journey he and Iowa wrestling have made together. When Gable arrived on the scene in Iowa City in 1972, the program had little to offer. J Robinson showed up as a volunteer assistant, asking for nothing other than the opportunity to work out with Gable and to be a part of the program, which was operating on a shoestring budget. Through hard work, long days, sweat and even tears of frustration, the program inched upwards. Because of Gable's reputation and the knowledge that under Kurdelmeier the Iowa program was offering opportunities to become involved, support was gained.

"The program was built around Gable and his love of the sport," said Jon Marks, a man who gave freely of his time in many capacities for many years before moving to Montana in 1983. "People who criticize the Iowa program and say they were handed all this stuff don't know what they are talking about. It was plain hard work by everybody, but work people wanted to do because they believed in Gable."

When Mark Johnson arrived from Michigan as a two-time All-American in 1979, he was hoping to catch some of the Iowa "magic." He had a high opinion of Gable, but was still amazed after being around him for some time. He soon felt he had discovered the "secret" to Gable's successes.

"It's simply this," said Johnson, a member of the 1980 Olympic team whom many consider the strongest wrestler, pound for pound, in the world. "Gable outworked everyone as a wrestler, and he outworks them as a coach. It's that simple."

Robinson is quick to agree.

"We try to establish a work ethic here," he said in the summer of 1984. "It's a work ethic that made America great, and a work ethic that makes Iowa great. We wouldn't ask any kid to do anything we wouldn't do ourselves. The secret to Iowa's success is work, work and then work some more. Sure, it's a big commitment, but it's one we all make, or should make, to be great."

The Iowa work ethic has made many a convert, including men like Chuck Yagla, Bruce Kinseth and Tom Burns. Yagla never won a state title, but managed to claim two NCAA titles and was named the Outstanding Wrestler in 1976, and also is the winningest wrestler in the history of the tough Midlands. He accomplished all that he did through plain hard work. He followed Gable's example, set high goals, committed himself to being the very best he could possibly be, and went for broke. So did Kinseth. As a senior at Decorah High School in Iowa, Kinseth won the state championship and junior national tournament in 1975, but received few scholarship offers. In the view of many, his skills were too limited for him to ever climb the mountain. Yet through plain hard work, he finished up in spectacular style, winning the 1979 Big Ten title with four straight pins, and the NCAA title with five in a row. He was named the Outstanding Wrestler of the NCAA tournament.

Burns came to Iowa City after a fine career at Colorado State University, where he had been Western Athletic Conference champion and an NCAA qualifier at heavyweight. A tall and well built 250-pounder, Burns had won over 50 matches in just two years at Colorado State, but felt he had not tapped his true potential. At Iowa he found what he was searching for. Though he left Iowa City in 1979 to pursue a career in teaching and coaching, the three years he spent at Iowa are special to him.

"Being a part of the University of Iowa wrestling program has had a tremendous affect on my life, both as an athlete and a person," said Burns in the spring of 1984. "Gaining success as a wrestler was my main reason for going to Iowa. But now that the competition is over, I find I have gained far more.

"The togetherness of the people, the intensity displayed in all parts of the program to make it what it is, are unbelievable. I feel that I not only gained personal success from being a small part of a great program, but so much of what I learned by being in the Iowa program has carried over into my professional life as a teacher and a coach."

Working with young, aspiring athletes as a teacher and coach (junior high wrestling and strength conditioning are his main areas) in Tulsa, Oklahoma, Burns fully realizes the invaluable lessons he learned at Iowa.

The poet Robert Frost wrote something many years ago which

Tom Burns of the Hawkeye Wrestling Club has Oklahoma State's three-time NCAA heavyweight champion Jimmy Jackson hopping during their 1979 match. Burns is just one of many athletes who came to Iowa City to become a better wrestler, and left with the feeling he had also become a better person. (Photo by Chuck Yesalis).

captures the essence of Gable's philosophy.: "The world is filled with willing people—some willing to work, the rest willing to let them."

So it is with Gable and the Hawkeyes. Men like Yagla, Kinseth and Burns were willing to adapt to a new philosophy, a new strategy, a new way of life, to become the best. What they, and others like them, have done is lay the groundwork for a new breed of wrestler—an athlete who goes all out, pays any price, accepts any workload, in his quest for supremacy. It's a new breed of athlete, one who is striving to emulate Gable himself, and to become the absolute best he can.

Conclusion

The Iowa wrestling program is a business of astounding success in the world of collegiate athletics. It may not be the greatest program ever, but there are those who claim it is near the very top. At least in our own time, our own wrestling world, it is the best we have. It is an example to follow and emulate in terms of structure, commitment, discipline, hard work and enthusiasm—if you chose to attain the pinnacle of success.

Whatever it has gained, it has earned. Those who would like to stand by its side have a choice. They must act now, to learn from Gable and his Hawks or to fall by the wayside, and be content with mediocrity. Too often, I hear of the Big Four—Iowa, Iowa State, Oklahoma State and Oklahoma—but the East has its Lehigh, Penn State, Syracuse and North Carolina. The West has its Cal Poly and Oregon and is developing San Jose State and Cal State-Bakersfield. These Schools have their champions, champions who are made, not bought.

Unfortunately those of us who love wrestling seem to be a vanishing species, struggling for survival along with the bald eagle. We need to bury the hatchet of verbal assault and work together, for the good of the sport we all love, struggling in unity to match the popularity of basketball and to defeat the Soviets in competition. We need to combine our resources and pool out talents in an effort to improve the quality of wrestling in the United States.

"A house divided against itself cannot stand," said a great man over a 100 years ago. Abraham Lincoln was speaking of the Union, of course, but he could have been referring to his favorite sport—wrestling—in the 1980s.

Each coach as a leader, must take up the challenge, and ask, in total honesty, if he is willing to make the necessary commitment. If the answer is "no," then move aside and watch others pass by on their way to the top of the mountain, chasing the Hawks. Men like Russ Hellickson of Wisconsin, Don Briggs of Northern Iowa, Joe Seay of Cal State-Bakersfield and Tommy Chesbro of Oklahoma State are not going to concede a thing to Iowa; they are hungry for the same sort of success, and are diligently in hot pursuit.

But I must caution you that success like Iowa's does not come easily, and you may become impatient with slow progress and

Jim Zalesky, in the midst of scoring a crunching takedown, personifies the new breed of Hawkeye wrestler. The graduate of Cedar Rapids Prairie High School closed out his illustrious career by scoring his 91st consecutive win at the NCAA championship of 1984. Zalesky also was a three-time Big Ten and three-time NCAA champion and posted a career record of 132 wins, seven losses and one tie. (Photo by Chuck Yesalis).

disillusioned with failure. Of course, no one ever said it would be easy. But stick to your goals, run the course with dedication and enthusiasm and after each season measure your success and evaluate your progress. Nothing comes overnight. It took Iowa sixty-two years to capture its first NCAA team title. Give yourself time and prepare for the future by working hard today.

America is blessed with plenty of talented athletes, and part of the responsibility of a coach is to locate those who will fit into his system. Talent is important, but Gable and his coaches look inside a person, trying to assess the levels of his desire and attitude. Iowa wants athletes who are committed, and will pay the price that men like Bruce Kinseth and Chuck Yagla have paid. The search will take long hours, plenty of travel, and the acceptance of wrestling as a year-round vocation.

Athletics teach us much about life—that life is a battle, and for the most part a one-on-one experience.

The lessons I have learned at Iowa will be with me the rest of my life. My message to you, the reader, is simple: Work hard and help others to become better. Unite in friendship and fellowship and help the wrestling community grow and prosper. That's the message from one of the new breed, and one who sincerely hopes that you will become a part of the new breed, too.

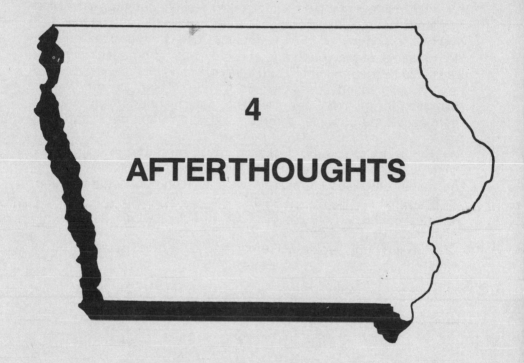

4
AFTERTHOUGHTS

To sum up my personality and my life in one book, let alone a few paragraphs, would be difficult; but here goes the old college try. I find myself a taster, a sampler of life—equally in athletics, academics, employment and friendhips. There seems to be a misconception that once we graduate from college, or get our first jobs, we are adults. I beg to differ.

I'm like a cake mixture—a little yolk, a little flour, a little milk, but not quite finished or mixed completely. I feel I'm constantly growing into a more complete person as the years pass by (and as hairs fall out) by allowing myself to experiment in, learn from and take part in life. I choose, at the young age of twenty-four, to be a jack of many trades, so to speak. Before I can fathom putting on the roof I need to have a solid foundation. I believe in not rushing life but, rather, searching for my inner self, my pace, and my needs, and meeting them as well as possible, compromising only when necessary and prudent.

By living this way, I feel many years from now all my "ingredients" will blend together well to form a more pleasing adult. I feel humans are like wine, and that we should only get better with age. As Benjamin Franklin once said, "Patience is a fine virtue for the young." By obeying his advice, I will, in the long run, become my master, my own person.

Finally, I hope people will remember me as a fellow who lived his way—not as a rebel, but as a maverick.

APPENDIX: THE
GABLE RECORD

Dan Gable was appointed head wrestling coach at the University of Iowa on August 24, 1976, after serving as Gary Kurdelmeier's assistant for four years. The Kurdelmeier-Gable team compiled a 51-7-5 record and won two NCAA team championships. Since taking over as head coach, Gable's record is an incredible 122-5-2 in dual meets, and he has won six straight NCAA team titles. He is the only man in history to win 100 matches as both a wrestler and a coach.

THE GABLE COACHING RECORD

In the Big Ten

	W	L	D	Rank
1977	7	0	0	1
1978	6	0	0	1
1979	7	0	0	1
1980	7	0	9	1
1981	9	0	0	1
1982	6	0	0	1
1983	6	0	0	1
TOTALS	47	0	0	100%

In All Competition

	W	L	D	NCAA
1977	17	1	1	3
1978	15	1	0	1
1979	19	0	0	1
1980	17	1	0	1
1981	21	1	0	1
1982	16	0	1	1
1983	17	1	0	1
TOTALS	122	5	2	94.6%

Champions Under Gable

	Big Ten Champs	NCAA Champs	All-Americans
1977	5	1	5
1978	6	0	6
1979	6	2	6
1980	4	2	8
1981	7	2	9
1982	7	3	8
1983	9	4	9
TOTALS	44	14	51

ABOUT THE AUTHORS

Lou Banach

Lou Banach came to the University of Iowa in the fall of 1978 after a tremendous high school career at Port Jervis, New York. In high school he was an all-state football player, state wrestling champion and a member of the National Honor Society. At Iowa, Lou became a two-time Big Ten and two-time NCAA wrestling champion, one of the most exciting and talented heavyweights in collegiate wrestling history. In the 1984 Los Angeles Olympics, Lou won the gold medal in the heavyweight division of the freestyle competition. Currently he makes his home in West Point, New York, where he is stationed as a lieutenant in the United States Army.